Discourses
at the
Communion
on Fridays

Indiana Series in the Philosophy of Religion

MEROLD WESTPHAL, EDITOR

Discourses at the Communion on Fridays

Søren Kierkegaard

TRANSLATED BY SYLVIA WALSH

Indiana University Press
Bloomington & Indianapolis

This book is a publication of

Indiana University Press
601 North Morton Street
Bloomington, Indiana 47404-3797 USA

iupress.indiana.edu

Telephone orders   800-842-6796
Fax orders   812-855-7931
Orders by e-mail   iuporder@indiana.edu

Library of Congress Cataloging-in-Publication Data

Kierkegaard, Søren, 1813–1855.
 [Discourses at the Communion on Fridays. English]
 Discourses at the Communion on Fridays / Søren Kierkegaard ; translated by Sylvia Walsh.
   p. cm. — (Indiana series in the philosophy of religion)
 Includes index.
 ISBN 978-0-253-35673-4 (cloth : alk. paper) 1. Lord's Supper—Lutheran Church. 2. Repentance—Lutheran Church. 3. Christian life—Lutheran authors. I. Walsh, Sylvia, [date] II. Title.
 BX8073.K5413 2011
 264'.36—dc22

                                                              2011005779

1 2 3 4 5 16 15 14 13 12 11

In Memory of Miyako, Julia, and Vanina

CONTENTS

ABBREVIATIONS

AN   Kierkegaard, *Armed Neutrality*. See entry below for *The Point of View* (PV)

ASKB   *Auktionsprotokol over Søren Kierkegaards Bogsamling*, ed. H. P. Rohde (København: Det Kongelige Bibliotek, 1967)

CA   Kierkegaard, *The Concept of Anxiety*, ed. and trans. Reidar Thomte in collaboration with Albert B. Anderson (Princeton, N.J.: Princeton University Press, 1980)

CD   Kierkegaard, *Christian Discourses* [and] *The Crisis and a Crisis in the Life of an Actress*, ed. and trans. Howard V. Hong and Edna H. Hong (Princeton, N.J.: Princeton University Press, 1997)

CI   Kierkegaard, *The Concept of Irony with Continual Reference to Socrates together with Notes on Schelling's Berlin Lectures*, ed. and trans. Howard V. Hong and Edna H. Hong (Princeton, N.J.: Princeton University Press,1989)

CUP   Kierkegaard, *Concluding Unscientific Postscript to "Philosophical Fragments,"* 2 vols., ed. and trans. Howard V. Hong and Edna H. Hong (Princeton, N.J.: Princeton University Press, 1992)

EUD   Kierkegaard, *Eighteen Upbuilding Discourses*, ed. and trans. Howard V. Hong and Edna H. Hong (Princeton, N.J.: Princeton University Press, 1990)

FSE   Kierkegaard, *For Self-Examination* [and] *Judge for Yourself!* ed. and trans. Howard V. Hong and Edna H. Hong (Princeton, N.J.: Princeton University Press, 1990)

FT   Kierkegaard, *Fear and Trembling*, ed. C. Stephen Evans and Sylvia Walsh, trans. Sylvia Walsh (Cambridge: Cambridge University Press, 2006)

IKC:CD   *International Kierkegaard Commentary*, vol. 17, *Christian Discourses and The Crisis and a Crisis in the Life of an Actress*, ed. Robert L. Perkins (Macon, Ga.: Mercer University Press, 2007)

IKC:EUD   *International Kierkegaard Commentary*, vol. 5, *Eighteen Upbuilding Discourses*, ed. Robert L. Perkins (Macon, Ga.: Mercer University Press, 2003)

IKC:FSE/JFY *International Kierkegaard Commentary: For Self-Examination
             and Judge for Yourself!* vol. 21, ed. Robert L. Perkins (Macon,
             Ga.: Mercer University Press, 2002)
IKC:PC   *International Kierkegaard Commentary,* vol. 20, *Practice
             in Christianity,* ed. Robert L. Perkins (Macon, Ga.: Mercer
             University Press, 2004)
IKC:SUD   *International Kierkegaard Commentary: The Sickness unto
             Death,* vol. 19, ed. Robert L. Perkins (Macon, Ga.: Mercer
             University Press, 1987)
IKC:TDIO   *International Kierkegaard Commentary,* vol. 10, *Three
             Discourses on Imagined Occasions,* ed. Robert L. Perkins
             (Macon, Ga.: Mercer University Press, 2006)
IKC:UDVS   *International Kierkegaard Commentary,* vol. 15, *Upbuilding
             Discourses in Various Spirits,* ed. Robert L. Perkins (Macon,
             Ga.: Mercer University Press, 2005)
IKC:WA   *International Kierkegaard Commentary,* vol. 18, *Without
             Authority,* ed. Robert L. Perkins (Macon, Ga.: Mercer
             University Press, 2007)
IKC:WL   *International Kierkegaard Commentary,* vol. 16, *Works of Love,*
             ed. Robert L. Perkins (Macon, Ga.: Mercer University Press,
             1999)
JFY   Kierkegaard, *Judge for Yourself!* See entry above for *For Self-
             Examination* (FSE).
JP   *Søren Kierkegaard's Journals and Papers,* 7 vols., ed. and trans.
             Howard V. Hong and Edna H. Hong, assisted by Gregor
             Malantschuk (Bloomington: Indiana University Press, 1967
             [vol. 1], 1970 [vol. 2], 1975 [vols. 3 and 4], and 1978 [vols. 5–7])
NB   Notebook in Kierkegaard's journals in SKS below
OMWA   Kierkegaard, *On My Work as an Author.* See entry below for
             The Point of View (PV).
PC   Kierkegaard, *Practice in Christianity,* ed. and trans. Howard
             V. Hong and Edna H. Hong (Princeton, N.J.: Princeton
             University Press, 1991)
PV   Kierkegaard, *The Point of View for My Work as an Author*
             [and] *On My Work as an Author* [and] *Armed Neutrality,* ed.
             and trans. Howard V. Hong and Edna H. Hong (Princeton,
             N.J.: Princeton University Press, 1998)

SKP   *Søren Kierkegaards Papirer,* 2nd enlarged ed., vols. 1–13,
ed. Niels Thulstrup, vols. 14–16 (index), ed. Niels Jørgen
Cappelørn (Copenhagen: Gyldendal, 1968–78)

SKS   *Søren Kierkegaards Skrifter,* ed. Niels Jørgen Cappelørn,
Joakim Garff, Jette Knudsen, Johnny Kondrup, and Alastair
McKinnon, 26 vols. (Copenhagen: Gads Forlag, 1997–)

SKS K   *Kommentar til Søren Kierkegaards Skrifter.* Commentary
volumes that accompany each text of *Søren Kierkegaards
Skrifter.* Each has the same volume number as the text it
accompanies in the new edition of SKS.

SUD   Kierkegaard, *The Sickness unto Death,* ed. and trans. Howard
V. Hong and Edna H. Hong (Princeton, N.J.: Princeton
University Press, 1980)

SV1   *Søren Kierkegaards Samlede Værker.* Edited by A. B.
Drachmann, J. L. Heiberg, and H. O. Lange. 1st ed. 14 vols.
(Copenhagen: Glydendalske Boghandels Forlag, 1901–1906)

TDIO   Kierkegaard, *Three Discourses on Imagined Occasions,* ed. and
trans. Howard V. Hong and Edna H. Hong (Princeton, N.J.:
Princeton University Press, 1993)

TM   Kierkegaard, *"The Moment" and Late Writings,* ed. and
trans. Howard V. Hong and Edna H. Hong (Princeton, N.J.:
Princeton University Press, 1998)

UDVS   Kierkegaard, *Upbuilding Discourses in Various Spirits,* ed. and
trans. Howard V. Hong and Edna H. Hong (Princeton, N.J.:
Princeton University Press, 1993)

WA   Kierkegaard, *Without Authority,* ed. and trans. Howard
V. Hong and Edna H. Hong (Princeton, N.J.: Princeton
University Press, 1997)

WL   Kierkegaard, *Works of Love,* ed. and trans. Howard V. Hong
and Edna H. Hong (Princeton, N.J.: Princeton University
Press, 1995)

Discourses
at the
Communion
on Fridays

Introduction

The sacrament of the Lord's Supper, Eucharist, or Holy Communion is regarded by many Christians as the central rite of the Christian religion. Yet in the history of Christian thought there is little liturgical literature, either dogmatic or popular, that focuses reflectively on the appropriate penitential posture for participation in this sacred ritual or on its personal import for the individual communicant who partakes of the holy meal. The publication of a series of communion discourses by the Danish philosopher of religion and Christian thinker Søren Kierkegaard (1813–1855) constitutes a unique contribution to the phenomenology of religion in this regard. Written with communicants of the Evangelical Lutheran Church of Denmark specifically in mind but potentially edifying for every individual regardless of his or her religious affiliation, Kierkegaard's communion discourses fill a major void in this genre of religious discourse.

Among his many religious and philosophical works, all produced in the course of little more than a decade, Kierkegaard wrote a total of thirteen discourses for the communion on Fridays, which was his favorite time to take communion in his native city of Copenhagen, where communion services were regularly held in Lutheran churches on Fridays, Sundays, and holy days.[1] Three of these discourses were actually delivered by Kierkegaard at the Church of Our Lady in the parish where he lived and worked as an independent author.[2] By his own admission, Kierkegaard wrote and spoke "without authority" since he was not an ordained minister or teacher, although he attended the pastoral seminary for a year after completing his undergraduate

1. Niels Cappelørn, "Søren Kierkegaard at Friday Communion in the Church of Our Lady," trans. K. Brian Söderquist, in IKC:WA, 259, 276–78.
2. Ibid., 283–85.

degree in theology at Copenhagen University and was later awarded
a magister or doctoral degree in philosophy by the same institution.
Nor did Kierkegaard claim to be an extraordinary Christian or truth-
witness who had suffered for the faith; he claimed only to be "a singular kind of poet and thinker" who sought in his writings to depict and
illuminate Christianity in its utmost ideality and integrity in the hope
that it might become an existential possibility for every human being.[3]

Of the thirteen communion discourses written by Kierkegaard,
twelve were published under the title "Discourses at the Communion
on Fridays" in groups of seven (Part IV of *Christian Discourses* in
1848), three (1849), and two (1851). The remaining communion discourse, which was delivered by Kierkegaard at a Friday communion
service in 1848, was published as the first of seven "Christian Expositions" that make up No. III, "From on High He Will Draw All to Himself," of *Practice in Christianity* (1850). All of these expositions, which
share the same or a slightly variant format consisting of an opening
prayer, biblical text, and exposition of the text, were originally intended to be communion discourses.[4] After much internal debate, however, Kierkegaard changed his mind because he had decided to publish
Practice in Christianity pseudonymously and therefore impersonally,
which was not in keeping with the personal character of a communion discourse.[5] With the exception of the one communion discourse
published pseudonymously as a Christian exposition in *Practice in
Christianity*, then, all of Kierkegaard's communion discourses were
published under his own name and unquestionably reflect his own
views. One other discourse, *An Upbuilding Discourse* (1850), was also
originally planned to be published as a communion discourse and
then as a Christian discourse before receiving its final designation as
an upbuilding discourse.[6] Numerous texts and initial drafts for other
communion discourses that were never written or completed were
also recorded in Kierkegaard's journals.[7] We are thus left with only
thirteen discourses that were actually published and/or delivered as
communion discourses in Kierkegaard's authorship.

3. JP 6:6390–91, 6497, 6511, 6521; WA, 165; AN, 129–30.
4. JP 6:6245.
5. JP 6:6417, 6487; SKP X 5 B 99, 101.
6. WA, 261.
7. JP 2:2001; JP 4:3917–23, 3925–26, 3936–37, 3942, 6:6359; SKP VIII 1 A 567,
628; SKP X 1 A 29; SKP X 2 A 60. See also IKC:WA, 286 and 287n103.

Since the communion discourses were published at different times and appear either independently or as part of other works in Kierkegaard's authorship, it has seemed appropriate to gather them into a single volume. There is precedence for such a compilation inasmuch as Kierkegaard's early upbuilding discourses, which were originally published in groups of two, three, and four discourses together over the course of two years (1843–44), were reissued in his lifetime in a single volume under the title *Eighteen Upbuilding Discourses*.[8] Bringing the communion discourses together, however, has necessitated a new translation of them into English. The present text is based on the first Danish edition of Kierkegaard's collected writings but also takes advantage of recent philological scholarship and annotations of biblical references and other sources in the commentary volumes that accompany the new Danish edition of Kierkegaard's collected writings.[9] Previous English translations of the communion discourses by Walter Lowrie and Howard and Edna Hong have also been consulted.[10] While sticking close to the Danish text and respecting Kierkegaard's idiosyncratic use of punctuation where feasible and felicitous,[11] this fresh translation seeks to preserve the inward passion and lyrical style of the original text as much as possible in another language.

For "That Single Individual"

There are basically three reasons for undertaking this project. First and foremost is the desire to make the communion discourses readily accessible as a whole to "that single individual" (*hiin Enkelte*), the spiritually concerned reader to whom all of Kierkegaard's writings are addressed. For Kierkegaard, the category of the single individual constitutes "the very principle of Christianity" and "the one single idea"

8. EUD, xxii.

9. See SV1 X:247–317; SVI XI:243–280; SVI XII:141–46, 261–90. See also SKS K 10:5–84, 216–69; SKS K 11:251–303; SKS K 12:7–111, 199–208, 327–86.

10. See Søren Kierkegaard, *Christian Discourses and The Lilies of the Field and the Birds of the Air and Three Discourses at the Communion on Fridays*, trans. Walter Lowrie (London: Oxford University Press, 1939), 253–309, 357–86; Kierkegaard, *Training in Christianity and the Edifying Discourse Which "Accompanied" It*, trans. Walter Lowrie (1941; repr., Princeton, N.J.: Princeton University Press, 1957), 151–56; Kierkegaard, *For Self-Examination and Judge for Yourselves! And Three Discourses 1851*, trans. Walter Lowrie (1941; repr., Princeton, N.J.: Princeton University Press, 1968), 1–15; CD, 247–300; PC, 151–56; WA, 109–44, 161–88.

11. See JP 5:5981, 5983–86.

of his life and thought.[12] In his view, however, this category applies to all human beings, not just to Christians, inasmuch as, religiously understood, every human being "is, can be, yes, should be" a single individual whose ultimate responsibility as a human being is to become conscious of existing as a single individual before God, who is the qualitative criterion and ethical goal for what it truly means to be a human being or self.[13] In a very real sense, then, every human being is the intended recipient of Kierkegaard's writings.[14] Although composed in a specifically Christian liturgical context, his communion discourses in particular offer spiritual edification for every individual who is earnestly concerned about his or her relation to God or the eternal.

The Movement and Telos of Kierkegaard's Authorship and Life

A second rationale for bringing Kierkegaard's communion discourses together in a single volume is that, according to his own testimony, the authorship as a whole "points definitively to" and "gathers itself together in" the "Discourses for Communion on Fridays," where it reaches its "decisive point of rest" at the foot of the altar.[15] Even though Kierkegaard wrote and published other works after this claim was made, most notably the newspaper articles and pamphlets that made up his final attack on Christendom in *The Moment* (1854–55), there is no indication that he ever changed his mind about the significance of the communion discourses for the authorship as a whole. As the final telos and unifying element of Kierkegaard's authorship, the communion discourses thus occupy a special place in the authorship and are crucial for understanding it as a totality. In *On My Work as an Author* (1851), Kierkegaard describes the movement of the authorship as progressing "*from* 'the poet,' from the esthetic—*from* 'the philosopher,' from the speculative—to the indication of the most inward qualification of the essentially Christian; **from** the *pseudonymous Either/Or*, **through** *Concluding Postscript*, with *my name as editor* **to** *Discourses at the Communion on Fridays*."[16] He further claims in this accounting

---

12. JP 2:1997, 2004, 2033, 2046.
13. OMWA, 10; UDVS, 127–37; JP 2:1997, 2004, 2007–2008, 2033, 2046, 2048; JP 5:5975; SUD, 79; EUD, 475 (SKP VIII 2 B 192).
14. JFY, 91.
15. WA 165 (translation modified); JP 6:6407, 6418, 6461, 6487, 6519.
16. OMWA, 5–6.

that "the authorship, regarded as a *totality,* is religious from first to last," inasmuch as the aim of the whole authorship is to make people aware of the religious or essentially Christian by casting it into reflection in such a way as to lead that single individual, his intended reader, back out of reflection into the simplicity of Christianity and the existential task of becoming a Christian.[17]

Kierkegaard began his work as an author with the pseudonymous publication of a number of esthetic or poetic works designed to establish a rapport with people by beginning where the majority of them are, namely living largely on the basis of their esthetic (from *aisthēsis,* the Greek word for sense perception) or natural inclinations and capacities for sensuous enjoyment without any higher sense of what it means to be a human being or a Christian.[18] By depicting the esthetic lifestyle under the guise of various pseudonyms and literary figures representative of that life-view and sphere of existence, Kierkegaard sought, like Socrates, maieutically or indirectly "to deceive people into the truth," as it were, by replacing the illusion that they already are Christians with the realization that they actually "have their lives in entirely different categories"; that is, "in esthetic or, at most, esthetic-ethical categories."[19]

Having indirectly described one way of becoming a Christian, namely by moving away from the esthetic, in his early pseudonymous writings, Kierkegaard next set out to show through another pseudonym, Johannes Climacus, in his major philosophical work, *Concluding Unscientific Postscript,* that one cannot *reflect* oneself into Christianity via philosophical speculation or a rational comprehension of Christian truth as claimed by Hegelian speculative philosophy and the theology of his day. According to the *Postscript,* which in Kierkegaard's view constitutes the turning point of the authorship, the issue of the whole authorship in an eminent sense is that of becoming a Christian, particularly what it means to become a Christian in the context of the ecclesiastical and socio-political established order of Christendom, where everyone is automatically assumed to be a Christian by virtue of having been born in a so-called Christian nation.[20] Over against a

17. Ibid., 6–7.
18. PV, 44–46. For a fuller discussion of the concepts of the esthetic and poetic in Kierkegaard's authorship, see Sylvia Walsh, *Living Poetically: Kierkegaard's Existential Aesthetics* (University Park: Pennsylvania State University Press, 1994), 18–20 and passim.
19. OMWA, 7; PV, 41–43, 53–54.
20. CUP 1:50–51; OMWA, 8; PV, 41, 55, 63, 88.

prevailing cultural climate in which the matter of becoming and continuing to be a Christian was taken lightly and as a matter of course,
Kierkegaard's strategy as a religious author was "to make clear what
in truth Christianity's requirement is" by dialectically pointing out its
rigor as well as its leniency in order to prevent the illegitimate appropriation of grace without works.[21] Assuming that, "like the empty jar
that is to be filled," his readers would then be receptive to the religious,
or at least would be compelled to become aware of what it is, Kierkegaard embarked on what has come to be characterized as his "second
authorship," the overtly religious and specifically Christian works issued either under his own name or that of his Christian pseudonym,
Anti-Climacus, who represents the essentially Christian on a higher
level than Kierkegaard himself existentially embodied.[22] Anti-Climacus thus could present what it means to be a Christian in the strictest,
most ideal sense in a way that Kierkegaard, who wrote without authority, could not.

The communion discourses also gave expression to and served
as the final resting point for Kierkegaard's own existential position
in relation to Christianity. Maintaining that his work as an author
was "the prompting of an irresistible inner need," Kierkegaard regarded his authorship as constituting his own religious upbringing
and development in what it means to be a Christian.[23] Describing
himself as a "poet of the religious" and more specifically as a "Christian poet and thinker," he sought to present "the ideal picture of
a Christian" so that it could appear once again as a task for every
human being, including himself.[24] Painfully conscious of his own
falling short in the actualization of this ideal, however, Kierkegaard
described himself as "a poet who flies to grace" and repeatedly characterized himself as a "penitent" in his own personal religious life.[25]
Although he attended communion only forty-one times in his short
life, reconciliation with God and Christ through the consciousness
and forgiveness of sin constitutes the centerpiece of both his theology and his life.[26]

21. OMWA, 16–17.
22. OMWA, 8; JP 6:6433.
23. OMWA, 12; PV, 24; JP 6:6533, 6786.
24. JP 6:6391, 6511, 6521; AN, 130–31. On Kierkegaard as a religious poet, see
Walsh, *Living Poetically,* 223–42.
25. SKP X 6 B 215; WA, 165; PV, 24; JP 6:6195, 6206, 6317, 6325, 6327, 6335, 6364, 6383.
26. IKC:WA, 261.

Types of Discourses in Kierkegaard's Authorship

A third reason for collecting the communion discourses into a single volume is that they form an important category or genre in their own right in the Kierkegaardian corpus and deserve to be considered as such.[27] Kierkegaard distinguished between several types of discourses in his authorship: **upbuilding or edifying discourses** (*Eighteen Upbuilding Discourses;* "What We Learn from the Lilies in the Field and from the Birds of the Air" in *Upbuilding Discourses in Various Spirits; An Upbuilding Discourse*); **occasional discourses** (*Three Discourses on Imagined Occasions;* "An Occasional Discourse" in *Upbuilding Discourses in Various Spirits*); **devotional discourses** (*The Lily in the Field and the Bird of the Air*); **Christian discourses** ("The Gospel of Sufferings" in *Upbuilding Discourses in Various Spirits; Christian Discourses; The Changelessness of God*); **Christian deliberations in the form of discourses** (*Works of Love*); **Christian discourses and expositions for upbuilding, awakening, inward deepening, and self-examination** ("Thoughts That Wound from Behind—for Upbuilding" in *Christian Discourses; The Sickness unto Death; Practice in Christianity; For Self-Examination; Judge for Yourself!*); and **communion discourses** (as identified above). The communion discourses can also be classified as a subcategory of Christian discourses (as in *Christian Discourses*), just as all of Kierkegaard's discourses and expositions can be seen as falling under the wider category of the upbuilding, whose aim is to build up the reader spiritually "from the ground up"; that is, upon the firm and deep foundation of love, which for Kierkegaard is "the deepest ground of the spiritual life" and what it means to build up and to be built up in the deepest sense.[28]

---

27. Ibid., 288–89. See also JP 6:6494, where Kierkegaard projects that the discourses for Fridays "can become a regular form of productivity" (translation modified).

28. WL, 210–16. On love as the dialogical basis of upbuilding, see Pia Søltoft, "To Let Oneself Be Upbuilt," in *Kierkegaard Studies Yearbook 2000,* ed. Niels Cappelørn, Hermann Deuser, Jon Stewart, and Christian Fink Tolstrup (Berlin: Walter de Gruyter, 2000), 19–39; and George Pattison, "A Dialogical Approach to Kierkegaard's Upbuilding Discourses," *Zeitschrift für Neuere Theologiegeschichte/Journal for the History of Modern Theology* 3 (1996): 185–202. On the category of upbuilding in Kierkegaard's writings, see George Pattison, *Kierkegaard's Upbuilding Discourses: Philosophy, Theology, Literature* (London: Routledge, 2002), 12–34; Søren K. Bruun, "The Concept of 'The Edifying' in Søren Kierkegaard's Authorship," in *Kierkegaard Yearbook 1997,* ed. Niels Jørgen Cappelørn and Hermann Deuser (Berlin: Walter de Gruyter, 1997), 228–52; and Harvie Ferguson, *Melancholy and the Critique of Modernity: Søren Kierkegaard's Religious Psychology* (London: Routledge, 1995), 185–209.

Upbuilding Discourses

Kierkegaard regarded the upbuilding or edifying as constituting *his* category as a poetic writer.[29] The discourses explicitly designated as upbuilding in his authorship were published under his own name and have their point of departure in the universally human or that which applies equally to every human being without regard to sex, class, age, education, or spiritual cultivation.[30] Although the early pseudonymous writings were offered to readers with his left hand and the series of upbuilding discourses that accompanied them with his right, Kierkegaard complained that "all or almost all took the left hand with their right," thereby missing the religious import of the upbuilding, which in his view was what should come to the fore and be stressed in the authorship.[31] While upbuilding discourses take the form of direct communications, which normally seek to convey knowledge of some sort to the reader, they are really indirect communications inasmuch as a general knowledge and understanding of the ethical-religious concepts discussed in them is presupposed in the reader.[32] Thus they seek only to "move, mollify, reassure, persuade" readers by prompting them to engage in self-examination in the context of their own particular, concrete situations in life on the assumption that, based on the spiritual equality of all persons before God, every individual possesses the capacity to actualize the universally human in his or her life.[33] Ideally, these discourses are meant to be read aloud so as to make the speaker's voice one's own and to transform the discourses into a conversation with oneself as well as indirectly with the author.[34] Kierkegaard was also careful to distinguish upbuilding discourses from sermons, which in his view operate "absolutely and solely" on the basis of scriptural and apostolic authority, whereas upbuilding discourses function "with the aid of reflection."[35]

---

29. JP 6:6431, 6438, 6461.

30. EUD, 240, 470 (SKP VII 1 B 220), 473–74 (SKP VIII 2 B 188), 475–76 (SKP VIII 2 B 192); JP 2:2033.

31. PV, 36; EUD, 179; JP 6:6238, 6519.

32. See JP 1:641, 648, 651, 653, 649.10, 651, 656; JP 6:6234.

33. EUD, 141–43; JP 5:5975; CUP 1:261. On Kierkegaard's early upbuilding discourses, see the essays in IKC:EUD; and in Cappelørn et al., *Kierkegaard Studies Yearbook 2000.*

34. EUD, 53, 231; JP 5:5981.

35. EUD, 5, 53, 107, 179, 231, 295; JP 1:207; UDVS, 386 (SKP VIII 1 A 21); CUP 1:272–73.

According to Johannes Climacus, the pseudonymous author of the *Postscript*, the early upbuilding discourses that make up the collected volume of *Eighteen Upbuilding Discourses* employ "only the ethical categories of immanence," which assume an eternal unity and continuity of the human with the divine and thus the possibility of knowing God within oneself apart from revelation.[36] Consequently, they give expression to what Climacus calls "Religiousness A," or immanent religiousness, in contradistinction to "Religiousness B," or Christianity, which is rooted in transcendence or a subjective relation to God via the paradoxical entrance of the eternal in time in the form of an individual human being, namely Jesus Christ.[37] Climacus rightly claims that "Christian truth as inwardness is also upbuilding, but this by no means implies that every upbuilding truth is Christian; the upbuilding is a wider category."[38] But Kierkegaard's early upbuilding discourses do presuppose and discuss a number of Christian concepts such as suffering, sin, repentance, forgiveness, salvation, faith, and love of the neighbor, although not in the strict sense in which they are later presented in his specifically Christian writings.[39] Likewise, *An Upbuilding Discourse* (1850), which was originally called a communion discourse and then a Christian discourse before receiving its final title, is quite Christian in orientation even though it is designated as an ethical-religious discourse.[40] Noting the commonality or universally human presence of sin and sins in everyone, this discourse presents the biblical figure of the woman who was a sinner in Luke 7:37–50 as a prototype of piety in the form of a silent teacher from whom we can learn the proper sorrow over our sins, our inability to do anything at all with regard to finding forgiveness, and (indirectly) the comfort we receive from the atonement of Christ.[41]

---

36. CUP 1:256, 272, 560–61. Strictly speaking, Climacus refers specifically to the upbuilding discourses of 1843, but his characterization is applicable to all of the early upbuilding discourses.

37. CUP 1:555, 559–61.

38. Ibid., 256.

39. On the relation of Kierkegaard's early upbuilding discourses to Climacus's characterization of the religion of immanence in CUP, see Thomas C. Anderson, "Is the Religion of *Eighteen Upbuilding Discourses* Religiousness A?" in IKC:EUD, 51–75.

40. WA, 261.

41. Ibid., 145–60.

Occasional Discourses

In 1844 Kierkegaard announced in his journal: "Now I am going to write occasional discourses instead of upbuilding discourses."[42] This observation indicates that he made a clear distinction between upbuilding discourses and occasional discourses, several of which he proceeded to write and publish as such, namely *Three Discourses on Imagined Occasions* (1845) and "An Occasional Discourse" (popularly known as "Purity of Heart") in *Upbuilding Discourses in Various Spirits* (1847). The first work is comprised of three discourses on the imagined occasions of a confession, a wedding, and a funeral, although Kierkegaard originally planned to include six occasional discourses in this volume.[43] According to the author, these discourses were created for imagined rather than actual occasions, since "in actual occasional discourses some things cannot very well be said because of the presence of specific persons."[44] While the occasions in this instance are a product of the author's imagination, in Kierkegaard's view it is the reader who actually makes it an occasion or brings the occasion along with him or her by supplying the meaning of the discourse in the inward appropriation of its content.[45]

"An Occasional Discourse" also focuses on the occasion of a confession and has the form of a confessional discourse but is described by Kierkegaard as a "preparatory meditation" for confession.[46] In it, "decisive self-activity" in the form of a willingness to listen and to engage in self-examination is likewise required of the reader.[47] Although this discourse is not addressed to the reader as a specific person, since he or she is unknown to the speaker, Kierkegaard claims that if the reader thinks about the occasion "very vividly," it will seem as if the discourse were speaking directly to the reader, who has the capacity "to will to listen in order to will to act accordingly," which every human being is capable of doing if he or she so wills.[48]

---

42. JP 5:5741.

43. Ibid., 5778; TDIO, 126 (SKP VI B 138). On this work see the essays in IKC:TDIO.

44. TDIO, 118 (SKP VI B 128).

45. JP 1:811; TDIO, 129 (SKP VI B 101).

46. UDVS, 373–74 (SKP VII 1 B 173; SKP VII 1 B 192:10).

47. UDVS, 122–23, 174 (SKP VII 1 B 192). See also Sheridan Hough, "'Halting is movement': The Paradoxical Pause of Confession in 'An Occasional Discourse,'" in IKC:UDVS, 37–51.

48. UDVS, 123.

Devotional Discourses

In addition to writing discourses in the form of upbuilding and occasional discourses, Kierkegaard composed three "devotional discourses" (*gudelige taler*) under the title *The Lily in the Field and the
Bird of the Air* (1849).[49] The lily and the bird were favorite subjects
of Kierkegaard, as they had already been discussed at length in Part
Two of *Upbuilding Discourses in Various Spirits* (1847) and Part One
of *Christian Discourses* (1848). Whereas the upbuilding discourses
from 1847 on this theme are subtitled "three discourses" and those
from 1848 "Christian discourses," these discourses are the only ones in
Kierkegaard's authorship that were subtitled "devotional discourses"
(although they were originally subtitled simply as "discourses").[50] *Upbuilding Discourses in Various Spirits* was also originally titled "Devotional Discourses" but was changed to its present title in the final
copy.[51] Like the other upbuilding and Christian discourses on this
theme, in these discourses the lily and the bird function immediately,
poetically, and humorously as the "divinely appointed teachers" of humankind, teaching us the contentment, glory, and blessed happiness
of being a human being, the difference between the Christian and the
pagan or ungodly person, and the art of becoming silent, unconditionally obedient, and unconditionally joyful before God.[52] However,
Kierkegaard points out in a journal entry that in alluding to the Lord's
Prayer in the third discourse, he avoided mentioning the petition
about the forgiveness of trespasses in it because "in that regard the lily
and the bird cannot be the teachers" of human beings.[53]

Christian Discourses

Kierkegaard also distinguishes between upbuilding discourses and
Christian discourses, which make their first appearance in the authorship as Part Three, "The Gospel of Sufferings/Christian Discourses," in
Upbuilding Discourses in Various Spirits (1847), followed by a whole volume of them in *Christian Discourses* (1848). Although these works are

49. WA, 1–45.
50. Ibid., 1, 198 (SKP X 5 B 4).
51. JP 5:5934 (SKS K 8:173, 183, 185).
52. UDVS, 159–212; CD, 3–91; WA, 1–45.
53. WA, 201 (SKP X 1 A 252).

the only ones specifically designated as Christian discourses in Kierkegaard's authorship, all discourses (including the communion discourses)
written after the introduction of this category fall under it in a general
sense, since from this point on all of Kierkegaard's writings are essentially Christian in character with the exception of *The Crisis and A Crisis
in the Life of an Actress* (1848), a little pseudonymous esthetic article intended to show that Kierkegaard remained esthetically productive after
publishing only religious works during the previous two years.[54]

Like upbuilding discourses, Christian discourses are not sermons
inasmuch as they deal "to a certain extent with doubt," whereas in Kierkegaard's view "it is neither more nor less than heresy to deal with
doubt in a sermon."[55] Christian discourses nevertheless affirm the authority of the Bible and the apostles, not as "something one has thought
out," as in an upbuilding discourse, but as "something commanded,"
and thus more rigorously than in an upbuilding discourse.[56] Whereas
a sermon requires an ordained minister, both upbuilding discourses
and Christian discourses can be delivered by a layperson. Yet "The
Gospel of Sufferings" in *Upbuilding Discourses in Various Spirits* was
originally conceived as a collection of sermons, and *The Changelessness
of God,* subtitled simply "A Discourse" (and thus somewhat ambiguous
as to how it should be classified), is referred to as a sermon in Kierkegaard's journals and was delivered as such at the Citadel Church in
1851, although it was not published until 1855, shortly before his
death.[57] Unlike upbuilding discourses, which stress the universally human, Christian discourses place their focus on the essentially Christian; for example, the consciousness of sin and forgiveness and the vol-
untary suffering, self-denial, joy, and obedience that characterize the
inverse dialectic of Christianity in contrast to the natural, worldly, pagan, merely human mentality.[58] While the upbuilding always appears
at first as terrifying and crushing from the "pain, strife, danger" of

54. PV, 30.
55. JP 1:638; UDVS, 215.
56. JP 1:207, 638; SKP VIII 1 A 21.
57. TM, 263, 267; JP 4:4890–91; JP 5:5945.
58. UDVS, 213–341; CD, 93–159; WA, 67; JP 1:760; JP 3:3329, 3349; JP 4:4289,
4666, 4680, 4696, 4782; JP 5:5997. On inverse dialectic in Kierkegaard's thought, see
Sylvia Walsh, *Living Christianly: Kierkegaard's Dialectic of Christian Existence* (University Park: Pennsylvania State University Press, 2005). On Christian discourses see also
the essays in IKC:UDVS, 199–348; IKC:CD, 13–297; and *Kierkegaard Studies Yearbook
2007,* ed. Niels Jørgen Cappelørn, Hermann Deuser, and K. Brian Söderquist (Berlin:
Walter de Gruyter, 2007).

coming to the consciousness of guilt and sin, the terror is transformed into the upbuilding by the consolation that one suffers only once or for a single moment in temporality, even if the suffering lasts for seventy years, whereas one is victorious eternally—which is precisely the point at which Christian upbuilding begins for Kierkegaard.[59]

Christian Deliberations

Christian deliberations or reflections (*Overveielse*) in the form of discourses, which constitute the type of Christian discourses that make up *Works of Love* (1847), are also distinguished from upbuilding discourses by the fact that they do not presuppose a knowledge of the qualifying concepts of Christianity and thus "must not so much move, mollify, reassure, persuade as *awaken,* provoke people and sharpen thought."[60] For example, Kierkegaard says that "an upbuilding discourse about love presupposes that people know essentially what love is and seeks to win them to it, to move them. But this is in fact not the case. Therefore the 'reflections' must first fetch them up out of the cellar, call to them, turn their comfortable way of thinking topsy-turvy with the dialectic of truth."[61] In Kierkegaard's view, then, Christian deliberations "ought to be a 'gadfly,'" employing irony as well as the comic in an impatient and high-spirited manner that makes their tone "quite different from that of an upbuilding or edifying discourse, which rests in mood."[62] For Kierkegaard, true upbuilding is identical to love, inasmuch as "'to build up' is exclusively characteristic of love" and is its "most characteristic specification," so that "wherever upbuilding is, there is love, and wherever love is, there is upbuilding."[63] Consequently, all upbuilding "in knowledge, in insight, in expertness, in integrity, etc., insofar as it does not build up in love, is still not upbuilding in the deepest sense."[64] Since love has its source in God and is deeply rooted in human beings, it is built up in others by presupposing and loving forth love in them.[65]

---

59. CD, 96–98; EUD, 344; JP 4:4594.
60. JP 1:641 (translation modified).
61. Ibid.
62. Ibid.
63. WL, 212, 214.
64. Ibid., 216.
65. WL, 8–9, 157, 217. See also M. Jamie Ferreira, *Love's Grateful Striving: A Commentary on Kierkegaard's "Works of Love"* (Oxford: Oxford University Press, 2001); IKC:WL; *Kierkegaard Studies Yearbook 1998,* ed. Niels Jørgen Cappelørn and Hermann Deuser together with Jon Stewart and Christian Tolstrup (Berlin: Walter de Gruyter, 1998).

Christian Discourses and Expositions for
Upbuilding, Awakening, Inward Deepening,
and Self-Examination

While the discourses designated as Christian discourses and Christian deliberations are signed by Kierkegaard, the presentation of the essentially Christian in the most rigorous and strictest sense is assigned to his Christian pseudonym Anti-Climacus, who is the "author" of *The Sickness unto Death* (1849), subtitled *A Christian Psychological Exposition for Upbuilding and Awakening,* and *Practice in Christianity* (1850), whose three numbers or parts are designated as (I) "For Awakening and Inward Deepening"; (II) "A Biblical Exposition and Christian Definition"; and (III) "Christian Expositions."[66] In his journals Kierkegaard reiterates that "the upbuilding is mine, not the esthetic, not that for upbuilding [*til Opbyggelse*] either, and even less that for awakening [*til Opvækkelse*]," since they present the ideality of the essentially Christian at a higher level than he personally embodied.[67] These two works are thus intended for building up the single individual by awakening him or her to the most decisive categories of Christianity—the consciousness of sin, the possibility of forgiveness, and the possibility of offense at Christ in his lowliness and loftiness as the paradoxical incarnation of God in the form of an individual human being. Although signed by Kierkegaard, *For Self-Examination* (1851) and *Judge for Yourself!* (written in 1851–52 but published posthumously) are also oriented toward the inward deepening of the single individual in their emphasis upon the rigorous side of Christianity, namely the need for works along with faith and grace by following Christ as the prototype for Christian existence.[68]

Although Part Three of *Christian Discourses* (1848), which was also published under Kierkegaard's own name, is titled "Thoughts That Wound From Behind—For Upbuilding," it constitutes the polemical element in a work that otherwise was intended to be as gentle as possible in its presentation of the essentially Christian. For that reason Kierkegaard agonized over the appropriateness of including these discourses "for upbuilding" in a collection of Christian discourses,

---

66. See JP 6:6436. See also IKC:SUD; IKC:PC; *Kierkegaard Studies Yearbook 1996,* ed. Niels Jørgen Cappelørn and Hermann Deuser (Berlin: Walter de Gruyter, 1996).

67. See JP 5:5686; JP 6:6431, 6433, 6461.

68. FSE, 2. See also IKC:FSE/JFY.

which in his view "should be given in an altogether milder tone."[69] Finally, however, he decided that without them "*Christian Discourses* is much too mild" and "for me truly not in character."[70] Even more important, he decided they had to be included because they provided a sharp and intense contrast to the fourth part of the book through the juxtaposition of "something like a temple-cleansing celebration" with "the quiet and most intimate of all worship services—the Communion service on Fridays."[71]

The Communion Discourses

Just as the distinctions Kierkegaard makes between the various forms of upbuilding and Christian discourses are not rigid or always upheld, the same can be said with respect to the communion discourses. As in the cases of upbuilding and Christian discourses, Kierkegaard distinguishes communion discourses from sermons, which in his view operate "absolutely and solely on the basis of authority" and thus presuppose presentation by an ordained minister.[72] It has been convincingly argued, however, that the communion discourses (*altergangstaler*) are in fact communion sermons (*altergangsprædikener* or *kommunionsprædikener*), the short sermons given by a priest, ordained catechist, or unordained theological candidate (such as Kierkegaard) immediately before communicants received communion at the Church of Our Lady.[73] Moreover, in jotting down texts for possible communion discourses in his journals, Kierkegaard sometimes refers to them as Friday sermons (*Fredags-Prædikener*) and sometimes as Friday discourses (*Fredags-Taler*).[74] The identification of the communion addresses as discourses rather than sermons in his published works thus clearly reflects Kierkegaard's idiosyncratic view of them in conformity with the claim that he wrote and spoke without authority.

It has also been convincingly argued that Kierkegaard's communion discourses were not confession discourses (*skriftetaler*)—that is,

---

69. JP 5:6110–11.
70. Ibid., 6112.
71. Ibid., 6121.
72. CD, 249; JP 1:638; JP 3:3477; SKP X 5 B 204.
73. IKC:WA, 276–77.
74. JP 1:311, 2:2001; JP 4:3917–23, 3925–26, 3928, 3933, 3936–37; JP 6:6359; SKP X 1 A 29; SKP X 2 A 60; SKS 20, NB2:146–48, 151–53, 167, 170, 202, 247, 256; SKS 20, NB 3:36; SKS 20, NB 4:17, 25, 142.

discourses intended for presentation at the confessional services held at Our Lady's Church in separate confessionary rooms immediately before the communion service on Fridays.[75] These services were held for the confession of sin (not privately to a priest in a confessionary box as in former times but secretly before God, although in company with other persons) in preparation for going to communion, as required by the royally authorized Danish *Prayer Book*.[76] At the confessional a short address (not a sermon) was given by the officiating priest, followed by the absolution or remission of sins by the laying on of hands.[77] Although Kierkegaard jotted down ideas for confession discourses in his journals,[78] as noted earlier he wrote only two discourses for the occasion of a confession, neither of which was intended for presentation at an actual confessional service or was considered to be a confession discourse as such. The question of whether the communion discourses are confession discourses arises because Kierkegaard seems to refer to one communion discourse as if it were a confession address in which the listener/reader is invited to confess in secret to God through the speaker's voice before proceeding to communion (57–58).[79] The context of the discourse as a whole, however, clearly indicates that the occasion for its presentation is at a communion service rather than a confessional service. The text states that the discourse is being given at a "divine service" centered on the altar, namely Holy Communion (58), whereas the confessional service was an independent ecclesiastical event that took place in a room separate from the sanctuary and was not part of the church service proper.[80] The text further states that no preaching is taking place on this day, which would be true at a confessional service but not at communion, since the communion addresses were in fact sermons. In another communion discourse, however, Kierkegaard contradicts himself with regard to the confessional service, claiming that "in the confes-

75. IKC:WA, 278–82. See also Michael Plekon, "Kierkegaard and the Eucharist," *Studia Liturgica* 22 (1992): 217.

76. IKC:WA, 265–69, 271–72.

77. Ibid., 267–72.

78. See JP 4:3953; SKP VI B 162, 164, 166, 169, 172. See also JP 5:5919, which indicates that Kierkegaard originally planned to call *Upbuilding Discourses in Various Spirits* "Confessional Discourses."

79. Numbers in parentheses in the text refer to the present translation of Kierkegaard's communion discourses.

80. IKC:WA, 281.

sional it is certainly the priest who preaches, but the true preacher is still the confidant [conscience] in your inner being" (139). However that may be explained, whether as a slip of the pen or for rhetorical purposes, other communion discourses make it abundantly clear that the discourses are intended for communion rather than confession, inasmuch as the latter is frequently referred to as having already taken place. Moreover, since Kierkegaard was not an ordained priest, he would not have been permitted to pronounce the remission of sin with the laying on of hands after giving a confession address as required of the officiating priest at a confessional service.

Although not technically identified as occasional discourses, Kierkegaard's communion discourses were in fact written for a specific occasion, namely Holy Communion, and even more specifically for Holy Communion on Friday, which was a day when most people were at work and thus not free to attend communion. To Kierkegaard, however, Friday was the most intimate and solemn of all times to go to communion, precisely because, unlike Sundays or holy days, when a large congregation would be gathered in the sanctuary, only a small group (usually about twenty-five at Our Lady's Church)[81] came to the Lord's house on that day. Moreover, they came not because they were commanded to do so, as on a holy day, but because they were impelled to come by an inner need (56). In Kierkegaard's view, there was also a kind of secretiveness in going to communion on Friday, for unlike a holy day, when it was assumed that everyone was on his or her way to church, it would not occur to anyone passing by that one was going to church on a Friday. There, in the quiet and solemn stillness of the sanctuary, away from the din of noise outside, the single individual wishes to be alone before God in order to seek the forgiveness of sin and to become reconciled with God and Christ, whereas on a festival day one wishes to be with others in order to worship, praise, and thank God (57).

The Consciousness and Confession of Sin

While a communion discourse is not a confession discourse, the confession of sin is nevertheless a prerequisite for receiving the forgiveness of sin in Christianity. The confession of sin thus constitutes a major

81. Ibid., 277.

topic in Kierkegaard's communion discourses. Two discourses in particular are devoted to a discussion of this requirement through a focus
on two biblical figures, "the tax collector" (Luke 18:13) and "the woman
who was a sinner" (Luke 7:47), who serve as models or prototypes for
the confession of sin. But the confession of sin presupposes the consciousness of sin, a concept that is explored in depth in *The Sickness
unto Death* but also figures importantly in the communion discourses
as well as in other Christian discourses. Whereas *The Sickness unto
Death* primarily tracks the consciousness of sin and its intensification
in despair and offense in the movement of the self *away* from faith
and forgiveness, the communion discourses indicate the movement of
the self *toward* faith through a further qualification of the consciousness of sin so as to become an anguished conscience or contrite heart
that condemns itself and sorrows over sin (79).[82] As Kierkegaard sees
it, this type of consciousness of sin is the way, indeed the only way,
that Christ draws a person to himself (123). Within the innermost
recesses of every human being's heart, he claims, there dwells a confidant or "privy preacher" who accompanies us wherever we go and
from whom we cannot hide our sins (137–38). This confidant is the
conscience, which according to Kierkegaard is the true preacher that
"speaks simply and solely about you, to you, within you" (139). But the
depth of sin in human beings is not something they can discover by
themselves; rather, it must be revealed to them by Christianity, which
teaches that "*sin* is the corruption of nations and of every human being" (44).[83] The consciousness of sin is thus impressed upon us in Kierkegaard's very first communion discourse through an imagined first-
person meditation on the part of the listener/reader, who is reminded
of "all the atrocities which human being has committed against human
being, enemy against enemy, alas and friend against friend, about violence and murder and bloodthirstiness and bestial cruelty, about all the
innocently and yet so cruelly shed blood that cries out to heaven, about
cunning and craftiness and deceit and faithlessness," and so forth, and
above all the opposition and "suffering of soul" Christ received from
sinners "by belonging to the fallen human race" (45). The consciousness

82. JP 3:2461. On the consciousness of sin and forgiveness in Kierkegaard's writings, see further Walsh, *Living Christianly,* 17–50. See also Niels Jørgen Cappelørn, "The
Movements of Offense Toward, Away From, and Within Faith: 'Blessed is he who is not
offended at me,'" in IKC:PC, 95–124.
83. See also PC, 61; CD, 102, 113, 123, 133, 143.

of sin may lead us to want to flee from evil and corruption, but that is not so easy to do inasmuch as "sin has a power of its own to resist" and "an outstanding balance to exact, a debt it wants to have paid by the sinner before it relinquishes him" (47). From a Christian standpoint, that debt is paid by Christ rather than the sinner, but before redemption can be experienced personally, every individual must engage in "earnest and honest self-examination" and make a private accounting to God in the confession of sin (74).

Confession, however, is not intended to burden us with guilt but rather to help us discard that burden (74). No one is forced to confess, nor is anyone condemned at the confessional; on the contrary, Kierkegaard points out that "there is no one who accuses you if you do not accuse yourself," since individual confessions are not heard by the officiating priest at the confessional service but are made in secret before God (74). The biblical figures of the tax collector and the woman who was a sinner serve as patterns of confession in this respect. Standing far off and alone before God with downcast eyes in the consciousness of his guilt and offense, the tax collector beats his breast and cries, "God be merciful to me a sinner!" (Luke 18:13). Likening confession to standing far off, casting one's eyes down, and beating one's breast, Kierkegaard observes that it is precisely in and through these self-accusatory actions that the tax collector inversely comes near to God and is lifted up and declared justified or in the right before God (106).[84] In like manner, the woman who was a sinner expresses the strongest sense of shame in the self-hatred with which she condemns herself in the open confession of her sin before Christ (109). Understood Christianly, however, to hate oneself is inversely the strongest expression for loving (Christ) much, for which the woman's sins are forgiven her. As Kierkegaard astutely observes, "Oh, nothing else rests as heavy upon a person as sin's heavy secret; there is only one thing that is heavier: to have to go to confession. Oh, no other secret is as frightful as the secret of sin; there is only one thing that is even more frightful: confession" (110). Yet the woman who was a sinner did not spare herself with any leniency or compassion. By openly confessing her sin in the house of the proud Pharisees who mocked her and by weeping at the feet of Christ in total self-forgetfulness,

84. On the tax collector as the paradigmatic communicant, see Sheridan Hough, "What the Faithful Tax Collector Saw (Against the Understanding)," in IKC:WA, 295–311.

she shows that she loves Christ more than her sin and therefore loves much, for "a perfectly honest, deep, altogether true, entirely unsparing confession of sin is the perfect love; such a confession of sin is to love much," Kierkegaard says (114). By her great love the woman who was a sinner thus becomes a pattern or eternal picture of confession that motivates us to follow her to the altar, so to speak; she goes at the head as our guide on the way to communion.[85] There all who are burdened and heavy laden with the consciousness of sin are invited by Christ to receive rest for their weary souls through the forgiveness of sin, the pledge of which is received individually at the altar but also must be made true individually by loving Christ much in the confession of sin (114).

The Invitation of Christ

For Kierkegaard, the most important biblical text relating to communion is the invitation of Christ in Matthew 11:28: "Come here to me all you who labor and are heavy laden, and I will give you rest" (49–54). This text is particularly fitting for communion at Our Lady's Church inasmuch as the phrase "COME UNTO ME" is inscribed below a marble statue of Christ that overlooks the altar in this church. Sculpted by the nineteenth-century Danish artist Bertel Thorvaldsen, this statue of Christ welcoming all with outstretched hands is an impressive figure which, according to one commentator, "had an immense influence upon Kierkegaard" and, as noted in the text below, is alluded to several times in the communion discourses.[86] But it is the invitation of Christ itself that is emphasized in the discourses. While the invitation is extended to everyone—all those who are troubled or heavy laden from lowly toil, heavy thoughts, care of others, doubt, privation, pain,

---

85. On the woman who was a sinner, see further Sylvia Walsh, "Prototypes of Piety: The Woman Who Was a Sinner and Mary Magdalene," in IKC:WA, 313–42; and Walsh, "Comparing Genres: The Woman Who Was a Sinner in Kierkegaard's *Three Discourses at the Communion on Fridays* and *An Upbuilding Discourse*," in *Kierkegaard Studies Yearbook 2010*, ed. Niels Jørgen Cappelørn, Hermann Deuser, and K. Brian Söderquist (Berlin: Walter de Gruyter, 2010), 71–90.

86. See Roger Poole, *Kierkegaard: The Indirect Communication* (Charlottesville: University Press of Virginia, 1993), 22, 233–47. On Thorvaldsen as an artist, see Else Kai Sass, "Thorvaldsen: An Introduction to his Work," in *Kierkegaard and His Contemporaries: The Culture of Golden Age Denmark*, ed. Jon Stewart, Kierkegaard Studies Monograph Series 10 (Berlin: Walter de Gruyter, 2003), 375–405. Oddly enough, however, Sass does not mention the statue of Christ in Our Lady's Church in this article.

recollections, hopelessness, and sickness as well as all those who are healthy and happy—Kierkegaard points out that the gospel requires us to labor and be heavy laden in a deeper sense, namely with the godly sorrow and heavy burden of the consciousness of guilt and sin, and to sigh repentantly over those actions, both hidden and revealed, by which we were led to commit an offense against God or another human being (51–52). Only the penitent or contrite heart that condemns itself—which is the only way a human being can be said to resemble God, namely not by direct comparison but inversely—draws near to him in the confession of sin (79). What leads the penitent sinner to accept the invitation of Christ at the altar is the promise of rest for the soul in the thought that there is forgiveness for sin and in the reassuring utterance that one is forgiven on the only basis there is for a penitent, namely that atonement has been made for one's sin by Christ (52).

Between the Confessional and the Altar

Presupposing a contrite consciousness of sin and a penitent confession of sin on the part of the listener/reader, then, the communion discourses specifically address the period between the confessional and the altar, giving us pause on the way to the altar for the expression of our need and heartfelt longing for reconciliation with God, the renewal of fellowship or communion with Christ through the forgiveness of sin wrought by his sacrificial death and atonement, and the renewal of our pledge of faithfulness to him (39, 74). Their purpose, therefore, is not to impart any new teaching, to engage in difficult investigations, or to impress Christian doctrines upon us but rather to remind us first of all of what was perhaps stirring inwardly within us when the longing for communion was first felt: a recollection of the many times God's gifts have been squandered in the past; the sheer vanity of everything earthly and temporal; the uncertainty of everything except death; the loneliness of every human being in the world; the fact that, humanly speaking, there is no one, not even God, to rely on; the corruption of every human being by sin and evil; the terrible atrocities and violence human beings have committed against each other; and the complicity of all, including ourselves, in bringing about the death of Christ, who is our only trustworthy friend in heaven and on earth (39–46). The more we abandon ourselves to these thoughts, Kierkegaard suggests, the more the longing for the eternal and a renewal of communion with Christ triumphs within us, leading us to partake of the Lord's Supper not out of habit or custom or accidental circumstance but with heartfelt longing, which in Kierkegaard's view is the only true godly or worthy entrance to this sacred meal (39).[87]

The Lord's Supper

The Lord's Supper, Holy Communion, or Eucharist (from the Greek *eucharistia*, meaning thankfulness or gratitude) is characterized in various ways in Kierkegaard's communion discourses.[88] It is described first of all as a meal in remembrance of Christ, the recollection of whom serves to increase the heartfelt longing within us for communion with him (47). Yet even to remember Christ, we—who would much rather dwell on the joyful than the sorrowful, the good days and happy times, while remaining ignorant of horrors that might make our happy lives gloomy and serious or our unhappy lives even more gloomy and serious—must be reminded by the one we want to remember, leading Kierkegaard to ask rhetorically and ironically: "Is this even a remembrance when the one who is to be recollected must himself remind the one recollecting!" (62). It is primarily Christ's abasement, suffering, betrayal, and innocent death of which we must be reminded by him at the altar—a scene of horror that is imaginatively and vividly recreated by Kierkegaard to remind us that this event is not finished, inasmuch as the whole human race, and thus each and every one of us, is implicated as an accomplice in the crucifixion of Christ (66). The remembrance of this night is enough for Kierkegaard, and hopefully for the listener/reader as well, to feel the need of an atoner more clearly than ever before and thus to seek refuge in him, the Crucified One. Nailed to the cross, Christ performs an even greater miracle than those he performed while wandering about in Judea, namely the miracle of love whereby, without doing anything, "he moves every person who has a heart" by his suffering and death (68). The Lord's Supper, then, is

87. For an excellent analysis of the heartfelt longing for communion, see Niels Jørgen Cappelørn, "Longing for Reconciliation with God: A Fundamental Theme in 'Friday Communion Discourses,' Fourth Part of *Christian Discourses*," in *Kierkegaard Studies Yearbook 2007*, 318–36.

88. For a more detailed discussion of the Eucharist as characterized in the first set of communion discourses, see David R. Law, "Kierkegaard's Understanding of the Eucharist in *Christian Discourses*, Part Four," in IKC:CD, 273–97.

not only a *meal of remembrance* but also the *meal of love* and the *meal of reconciliation* instituted by Christ on the night he was betrayed in repayment for his betrayal, the most painful blow that can be inflicted upon love (67–68). Since in Kierkegaard's view it is the whole human race that has betrayed him, all of us, without exception, stand in need of this meal of love and reconciliation, which is a sign of God's incomprehensible compassion, greatness, mercy, and love in reconciling himself with the fallen human race by forgiving the world's sin (76, 78, 82).

Kierkegaard also describes the Lord's Supper as a *meal of blessing*, inasmuch as "there is always something missing in every meal if the blessing is lacking" and it would not exist at all if Christ had not blessed it (83). Even in our ordinary endeavors in life, Kierkegaard points out, we need God's blessing in order to undertake anything at all, regardless of whether it succeeds or not, as the more we have to do with God, the more we realize that we are not capable of doing anything at all without his blessing (85). At the altar, as sinners, we are capable of doing less than nothing to atone or make satisfaction for our sins, and thus we feel the need for a blessing all the more deeply (85). At the altar, however, Christ not only blesses the elements that are eaten and drunk, making the meal itself a blessing, but he *is* the blessing, so that in partaking of the bread and wine we partake of the blessing which is Christ himself, who is personally present, albeit invisibly, at the altar and in the elements (86).[89]

The Real Presence of Christ

In claiming Christ's real presence at and in the Lord's Supper, Kierkegaard reflects the Lutheran doctrine of consubstantiation, which holds that Christ is substantially or bodily present in, with, and under the bread and wine (which nevertheless remain bread and wine) in an incomprehensible, spiritual mode of presence.[90] Historically, this doctrine was formulated in direct opposition to the Roman

89. See also JP 6:6495.
90. *The Book of Concord: The Confessions of the Evangelical Lutheran Church*, ed. Robert Kolb and Timothy J. Wengert, trans. Charles Arand, Eric Gritsch, Robert Kolb, William Russell, James Schaaf, Jane Strohl, and Timothy J. Wengert (Minneapolis, Minn.: Fortress Press, 2000), 44–45, 184–85, 320, 362, 467–70, 505–506, 599, 591–615.

Catholic doctrine of transubstantiation, which claims that the physical elements are transformed into the very body and blood of Christ, as well as against Crypto-Philippist (Melanchthonian) and Reformed (Zwinglian and Calvinist) factions in Protestantism that deny the bodily presence of Christ in the elements.[91] As noted above, however, Kierkegaard is not interested in expositing Eucharistic doctrines in the communion discourses but rather in concentrating our attention on Christ's real presence at the altar—not only in the elements themselves but audibly as well. At the altar, he contends, "what is essential above all is to hear *his* voice," for if we do not hear his voice there, we go to communion in vain (58). Thus, when the invitation is given, it must be his voice that invites us, and when he says, "this is my body," it must be his voice that we hear. Unlike Sunday and holy day services, which center on the pulpit and the preaching of sermons that bear witness to the life of Christ and proclaim his words and teachings, the communion service centers on the altar, where "there is no speaking about him; *there* he himself is personally present, it is he who speaks—if not, then you are not at the altar," for the altar is the altar only if he is present (58). Physically speaking, of course, the altar is still there, but spiritually understood it is there only if his voice is heard there and one is known by Christ, who does not know those who do not hear his voice. By the same token, however, those who hear his voice are known by him as his own and follow him, which means that when they leave the altar, he accompanies them wherever they go (60). The altar, as it were, accompanies them as well, for wherever Christ is, there the altar is. "It is not then as if everything were therewith decided by someone going to communion on rare occasions; no, the task is, on leaving the altar still to remain at the altar," Kierkegaard observes (60). In this way the whole of the Christian life becomes one of communion with Christ. With regard to the Lord's Supper, he thus concludes in the last communion discourse: "It is not merely in remembrance of him, not merely a pledge that you have communion with him, but it is the communion, this communion that you then must strive to preserve in your daily life by living more and more out of yourself and identifying yourself with him, with his love, which hides a multitude of sins" (143). This passage echoes the ending of the first discourse, which reminds the

91. Ibid., 321, 504, 507–508, 592–94, 599.

listener/reader that Christ is not dead but alive and that you must "truly live in and together with him, he must indeed be and become your life, so that you do not live yourself, no longer live yourself, but Christ lives in you" (48).

The Atonement of Christ

For Kierkegaard, reconciliation with God and Christ is made possible through the atoning death of Christ, which is proclaimed at the altar in contrast to the pulpit, where it is primarily Christ's life that is proclaimed (142). In the Christian tradition, the act of Christ's atonement or making amends for the sins of the world by his death has been understood in several different ways.[92] The first way, known as the classic or dramatic theory, explains the atonement in terms of a cosmic battle between God and Satan, under whose evil power the world is held in bondage. According to this theory, God offered the death of Christ as a ransom or payment to Satan in order to free humankind from sin, death, and evil. The second way, called the Latin or legal theory, views Christ's death as making satisfaction for sin not to Satan but to God, whose divine honor and justice require that a penalty be paid for the transgressions of humankind in order to secure the remission or forgiveness of sin. A variant of this theory, called the sacrificial theory, views Christ as both the High Priest and sacrificial victim who acts as the representative of and substitute for human beings in making a sin-offering by his death in order to expiate (atone for) rather than to propitiate (appease God for) the sins of the world. A third (or fourth) way of understanding the atonement of Christ, variously described as the exemplar, subjective, or moral influence theory, emphasizes the role of Christ as an example whose humility, love, forgiveness, suffering, and death stir the hearts of human beings, leading them to repent of their sins and to love Christ and others in response.

With the exception of a brief discussion of the doctrine of the atonement in *Two Ethical-Religious Essays* (1849), which ponders the

---

92. For a detailed discussion of the main types of atonement theory, see Gustaf Aulén, *Christus Victor: An Historical Study of the Three Main Types of the Idea of the Atonement* (London: Society for Promoting Christian Knowledge, 1950). On Kierkegaard's view of the atonement, see also Sylvia Walsh, *Kierkegaard: Thinking Christianly in an Existential Mode* (Oxford: Oxford University Press, 2009), 132–37.

theological question of how Christ could have let human beings become guilty of putting him to death and concludes that "his death is
the Atonement for his death," and a brief discussion of the comfort
the atonement brings to believers in *An Upbuilding Discourse* (1850),[93]
the communion discourses are the only place in Kierkegaard's authorship where the significance of the atonement for the single individual
is actually spelled out. This alone seals their importance in the Kierkegaardian corpus. Even though Kierkegaard stresses Christ's role
as the prototype for Christian existence in his second authorship or
specifically Christian writings, in his view "the Atonement and grace
are and remain definitive" and "unconditionally needed," so that by
the atonement of Christ "the saved might at every moment find the
confidence and boldness to want to strive to follow [him]."[94] As early as 1847 and 1848 Kierkegaard envisioned writing discourses or a
book on the atonement, alternatively to be entitled "Work of Love,"
"Thoughts That Cure Radically, Christian Healing," or "The Radical
Cure or The Forgiveness of Sins and the Atonement."[95] Kierkegaard
partially realized this plan with the publication of *The Sickness unto
Death* (1849) and *Practice in Christianity* (1850), using his Christian
pseudonym Anti-Climacus. But it was not until the publication of the
last series of communion discourses in 1851 that it was fully realized,
although in a different and more appropriate genre than was first envisioned and, significantly, issued under his own name rather than with
a pseudonym.

Just as Kierkegaard is not interested in expositing dogmatic theories about the real presence of Christ in the communion discourses, he
likewise is not interested in trying to comprehend or explain the mystery of the atonement, which in his view cannot be comprehended but
must be believed. Rather, his focus is on the personal meaning of the
atonement for the believer or single individual who seeks reconciliation with God and Christ at the altar. It is in this intensely personal
and liturgical context, therefore, that his understanding of the atonement is set forth. This is not to say, of course, that his thought is not
informed or influenced by one or more of the traditional theories of

---

93. WA, 58–66, 158–60. See also CI, 314–17, where Kierkegaard engages in a critique of Solger's view of the atonement. The atonement is also mentioned sporadically
in other works by Kierkegaard, e.g., CA.
94. JP 2:1909; JFY, 147. See also Walsh, *Kierkegaard: Thinking Christianly,* 137–39.
95. JP 5:6092, 6110; JP 6:6210.

atonement as opposed to others. Clearly, Kierkegaard does not understand the atonement in terms of the classic theory of atonement as an
objective, impersonal, cosmic event in which a transaction takes place
between God and Satan to free us from the bondage of sin and evil.
Nor does he view it as a past event that is "over and done with." Rather,
he views it as a present event in which we are not merely spectators
but accomplices, inasmuch as it is the whole human race, to which all
of us belong, that is responsible for his death (65–66). In line with the
Latin theory, however, Kierkegaard does view Christ's death on the
cross as a sacrifice that makes repayment or satisfaction for the sins
of the world and for his crucifixion, but he understands this sacrifice
in a more personal manner as being offered "not for human beings in
general" nor "to save human beings in general" but "to save each one
individually" (59). What is emphasized in the communion discourses,
therefore, is the fact that Christ died "also for you," giving voice to
the listener/reader's own imagined self-reflection in the expression of
longing for the renewal of fellowship with him who has made satisfaction not only for "my every slightest actual sin, but also for the one
that perhaps lurks deepest in my soul without my being aware of it"
(47).

Kierkegaard also stresses that we are incapable of doing anything
at all with respect to making satisfaction for our sins, not even so
much as to make ourselves receptive to the blessing of Christ's atoning work by holding fast the thought of our unworthiness and need of
grace and blessing (85–86).[96] "If at the altar you want to be able to do
the least thing yourself, even merely to step forward yourself," he says,
"then you upset everything, prevent the atonement, make the satisfaction impossible" (86). With respect to the divine work of atonement,
then, Christ must do everything, the sinner nothing or less than nothing. Nowhere is this more poignantly expressed in the communion
discourses than in the discourse on the woman who was a sinner. Just
as she was literally able to do nothing at all to merit the forgiveness of
her sins, Christ is able to do absolutely everything in that regard (111).
Yet it was precisely in the impotence of literally being able to do nothing at all that inversely she gave the most powerful expression of the
truth that she loved Christ much.

96. See also Lee C. Barrett, "Christ's Efficacious Love and Human Responsibility: The Lutheran Dialectic of 'Discourses at the Communion on Fridays,'" in IKC:CD,
251–72.

Exactly how Christ atones for our sins is described in two ways
in the communion discourses. Reflecting the variant sacrificial theory
of atonement, Kierkegaard first views Christ's work of atonement in
terms of the High Priest of the New Testament Epistle to the Hebrews
who is able not only to sympathize with our human weaknesses but
also to put himself entirely in our place (93–99). The common complaint of sufferers and persons tested by temptation and spiritual tri-
als, Kierkegaard observes, is that no one is able to understand their
sufferings, sympathize with them, or console them because no one
can put him/herself entirely in their place (91, 96). In response to
this complaint Kierkegaard maintains that, unlike human sympathy,
Christ is able to put himself entirely in their and our place in several
ways and thus is able to offer true, divine sympathy and consolation
to all sufferers regardless of the nature of their sorrows. Christ puts
himself in our place first of all by becoming a human being like us
and then by becoming the human being who has suffered infinitely
more than any other human being ever has or ever will suffer (93). He
has been tested and tempted in all things in like manner to us yet has
endured every temptation without sin, which is the only respect in
which he does not and cannot put himself entirely in our place (98).
Not only was he the greatest sufferer but he was also the only sufferer
of whom it is veritably true that his only consolation was to console
others (95). Here, Kierkegaard contends, suffering reaches its highest
point but also its limit, where everything is inverted and Christ becomes "the Consoler" who is the only one of whom it holds true that
no one can put himself in his place while conversely he is the only one
who is able to put himself entirely in our place (95). In the atonement
Christ puts himself entirely in our place by replacing us and acting as
our deputy or substitute, suffering the punishment of sin in our place
so that we may be saved, and suffering death on the cross so that we
may live (99). For Kierkegaard, this is precisely what the satisfaction
of atonement means, namely that we step aside and Christ takes our
place, thereby putting himself entirely in our place:

> For what is the "Atoner" but a substitute who puts himself
> entirely in your place and in mine; and what is the consolation of
> the atonement but this, that the substitute, making satisfaction,
> puts himself entirely in your and in my place! So when punitive
> justice here in the world or hereafter in the judgment seeks the
> place where I the sinner stand with all my guilt, with my many
> sins—it does not find me; I no longer stand in that place, I have

left it, another stands there in my place, another who puts himself
entirely in my place. (99)

The bread and wine, Christ's holy body and blood, received at the altar
are the eternal pledge that Christ has done just that.

The second way of expressing what happens in the atonement in
the communion discourses is to say that Christ hides or covers a multitude of sins by his sacrificial death. Focusing on the passage from 1
Peter 4:8, "love will hide a multitude of sins," as it applies specifically
to Christ's love, Kierkegaard observes that only Christ has the divine
authority to hide our sins (140).[97] This no other human being can do,
least of all ourselves, as the voice of conscience within us prevents us
from hiding our sins from ourselves yet makes us feel the need to find
such a hiding place:

> Oh, that I knew how to flee to a deserted island where no
> human being ever came or comes; oh, that there were a place of
> refuge where I likewise could flee, far away from myself; that there
> were a hiding place where I am so hidden that not even the con-
> sciousness of my sin can find me; that there were a boundary, even
> if ever so narrow, if it still makes a separation between my sin and
> me; that on the other side of a yawning abyss there were a spot,
> even if ever so small, where I could stand while the consciousness
> of my sin must remain on yonder side; that there were a forgive-
> ness, a forgiveness that does not make my sense of guilt be in-
> creased but truly takes the guilt from me, also the consciousness
> of it; that there were an oblivion! (139)

The most a loving person, even the most loving person, can do, Kierkegaard claims, is to mitigate our guilt in our own eyes so as to hide it
from ourselves to a certain degree. But we cannot actually or literally
hide our guilt from ourselves "so that it is hidden like what is hidden
at the bottom of the sea . . . hidden so that what was red like blood
becomes whiter than snow, hidden so that sin is transformed into purity and you yourself dare to believe yourself justified and pure" (140).
Only Christ's love can do that. Christ *quite literally* hides our sin with
his holy body and in this way makes satisfaction for our sin by entirely
covering our guilt and making it impossible to be seen externally or

---

97. See EUD, 55–78, and WL, 280–99, where this theme is explored with reference to the expression of Christian love by the followers of Christ.

internally (140–41). Like the mother hen who is concerned to hide
her chicks under her wings in a moment of danger, protecting them
even to the point of laying down her life for them, Christ hides and
covers our sin in the same way, laying down his life in order to secure
a hiding place for us under his love (141). But whereas the death of
the mother hen ultimately deprives her chicks of their hiding place,
Christ covers our sins precisely by his death, since death can take away
a living person but cannot take away a dead person, making it therefore impossible for us to be deprived of our hiding place (141). From
Kierkegaard's perspective, therefore, there may be many works of love
but there is only one work that is the work of love or good work, which
is Christ's atoning death. Only by remaining in him and identifying
with him are we under cover and is there a cover over the multitude
of our sins (143).

Loving Much, Loving Little

Christ's pledge of the forgiveness of sin as a sign that Christ gives
himself as a cover for our sins constitutes the gospel's lenient word of
consolation that is heard and received at the altar, providing rest for
the troubled soul in the consciousness of the forgiveness of sin and in
the realization that even if we are unfaithful Christ remains faithful
in death as our savior and trusted friend who does not become weary
of forgiving (44, 71–73). Just as his unchanged faithfulness is forgiveness for the penitent, however, it becomes a punishment and curse
for those who deny him or take his faithfulness in vain. Although it
is primarily the gospel's lenient word of consolation that is heard at
the altar, both law and gospel, strictness and leniency are to be found
there. On leaving the church after receiving communion, therefore,
Kierkegaard imagines those persons who are not sensible of having
received forgiveness of all their sins as seeing an inscription from Luke
7:47 over the church door inside that reads, "[the one] to whom little
is forgiven loves little." For Kierkegaard, this constitutes both a word
of judgment and a word of consolation to the communicant (129). It
is first of all a word of judgment because the fault or responsibility for
the lack of forgiveness belongs not to the Holy Communion but to the
communicant him/herself. Just as the sins of the woman who was a
sinner were forgiven her because she loved Christ much, one is forgiv-
en little when one has loved him little. Kierkegaard points out that it is
a difficult matter to receive the forgiveness of sins rightly at the altar,

for unless the promise of forgiveness is heard rightly, so that we take the forgiveness of all our sins "quite literally" and cast them all away, even the recollection of them, and depart from the altar "as light of heart as a newborn child, upon whom nothing, nothing weighs heavily," we will go away not entirely relieved and possibly feeling even more oppressed by a sense of unworthiness to receive communion (128). Rare indeed is the individual who is able to feel "entirely relieved of every—even the least sin, or of every—even the greatest sin" and to succeed "to perfection" in experiencing the joy and blessing of communion (128–29). Yet it is not the severe judgment of justice that denies forgiveness because our sins are too great and too many but the even more severe judgment of love that says we are forgiven little because we have loved little. Ordinarily it is the judgment of justice that is thought to be severe, whereas love is lenient and does not judge, or if it does, is lenient in its judgment (129). But the lenient judgment of love, which declares that everything is forgiven, is changed into the most frightful severity by the self-inflicted judgment of being forgiven little because one has loved little—a sin of which we are all more or less guilty, Kierkegaard observes (131–32).

In keeping with the gospel, however, Kierkegaard points out that a word of consolation is also to be found in the statement that the one to whom little is forgiven loves little. Consolation can be had first of all from the fact that nothing is said about divine love in the text but only something about our love, which indicates that God's love is unchanged. Second, the text does not say that one is forgiven little because one has *loved* little in the past but because one *loves* little in the present, which means that there is always a possibility of change in the next instant to a different time in which one strives to love much.

The Blessed Recurrence of Salvation in Love

The forgiveness of sin on the basis of whether one loves much or little gives rise to the disquieting question of whether forgiveness is after all merited in Christianity. Kierkegaard himself poses this question in the last communion discourse, not with respect to *works,* as the issue is traditionally raised and discussed in Christian theology, but in relation to *love,* namely whether "it is love that makes the decision whether and how one's sins should be forgiven" (133–34). Kierkegaard answers this question with an emphatic "no," pointing to the parable of two debtors in Luke 7:41–43—one of whom owed much, the other little, but both of whom had their debts cancelled—as an illustration of Christ's teaching that forgiveness is not dependent on how much one owes or on one's ability to repay a debt, yet the person who is forgiven the most should love the most in return. Regardless of whether one is forgiven much or little, however, everything remains within the sphere of love and is prevented from entering "the hapless region of merit" by what Kierkegaard calls "the blessed recurrence of salvation in love," in which love and forgiveness stand in a reciprocal as well as proportional relation to one another, each eliciting and strengthening the other (134). First one loves much and is forgiven much; then the fact that one is forgiven much "loves forth love" again and makes it even stronger the second time, just as faith, which requires one to believe in order to be saved, becomes twice as strong after one is saved (134).

At the Foot of the Altar

The central dialectic of Christian existence for Kierkegaard is between the consciousness of sin and the forgiveness of sin, which presupposes an anguished conscience and contrite confession of sin on the part of the single individual in order to receive the pledge of forgiveness and reconciliation with God that is wrought through Christ's sacrificial atonement for the sins of all but each one individually. The place where these dialectical counterparts come together is in the service of Holy Communion. There the single individual's heartfelt longing for the renewal of communion with God and Christ hopefully finds satisfaction, consolation, and rest for the soul in the consciousness, confession, and forgiveness of sin. Inasmuch as Kierkegaard's communion discourses describe this dialectical moment and seek to prepare the reader for it, they command a central place in his authorship and play a decisive role in bringing it to its point of concentration and culmination at the foot of the altar. In the preface to the last series of communion discourses, Kierkegaard writes:

> A gradually advancing author-activity that began with *Either/Or* seeks here its decisive point of rest at the foot of the altar, where the author, personally most conscious of his own imperfection and guilt, by no means calls himself a truth-witness but only a singular kind of poet and thinker who, "without authority," has had nothing new to bring but "has wanted to read through once again, if possible in a more inward way, the original text of the

individual human existence-relationships, the old, familiar text handed down from the fathers." (125)

Following the lead of Kierkegaard's authorship, we are now invited by Kierkegaard's communion discourses to take up our own positions as single individuals at the foot of the altar, pausing only long enough to make the words of the author individually our own in the inward appropriation of them for the purpose of spiritual reconciliation and upbuilding in the context of our own religious affiliations and personal situations in life.

PART ONE

" Discourses at the Communion on Fridays," Part Four of *Christian Discourses* (1848)

Preface

Of these discourses, which still lack something essential to be and therefore are not called sermons, two (II and III) were delivered in the Church of Our Lady.[1] Even if he is not told, the knowledgeable reader himself will no doubt readily recognize by the form and treatment that these two are "delivered discourses," written to be delivered, or written as they were delivered.

February 1848   S. K

---

1. According to Kierkegaard's journals (SKP VIII 2 B 108), no. III was delivered at the Church of Our Lady on August 27, 1847. No date is given for no. II.

[1]

Luke 22:15

Prayer

Father in heaven! We know well that you are the one who enables both willing and completing[1] and that longing, when it draws us to renew communion with our Savior and Atoner [*Forsoner*],[2] is also from you. But when the longing lays hold of us, oh that we may also lay hold of the longing; when it wants to carry us away, that we may also abandon ourselves; when you are near to us in the call, that we may also keep near to you in supplication; when you offer the highest in the longing, that we may also buy its opportune moment,[3] may hold it fast, sanctify it in quiet hours by earnest thoughts, by pious resolves, so that it may become the strong but also well-tested heartfelt longing that is required of those who worthily want to partake of the holy meal of the Lord's Supper! Father in heaven, the longing is your gift; no one can give it to himself, no one can buy it if it is not given, even if he were willing to sell all[4]—but when you give it, then he can surely sell all in order to buy it. So we pray for those who are gathered here that they may go up to the Lord's table today with heartfelt longing and that when they leave there, they may go away with increased longing for him our Savior and Atoner.

---

1. See Philippians 1:6, 2:13.
2. This term is generally translated as "Redeemer" but in Danish it is the nominal form of *forsoning*, which means "atonement" or "reconciliation," and in the communion discourses it refers specifically to Christ as the one who makes atonement or satisfaction for sin through his death on the cross.
3. See Colossians 4:5; Luke 22:6.
4. See Matthew 13:44–46.

Luke 22:15: I have heartily longed to eat this Passover with you before I suffer.

The sacred words just read, which are Christ's own words, undoubtedly do not belong to the institution of the Lord's Supper, yet in the narrative they stand in the closest connection with it; the words of institution follow immediately after these words.[5] It was on the night when he was betrayed, or rather he was already betrayed, Judas was already bought to sell him and had already sold him;[6] the betrayer now sought only the "opportune time, so that he could betray him to the high priests without a crowd" (Luke 22:6).[7] For that he chose the stillness of the night in which Christ now for the last time was gathered with his apostles. "And when the hour came he sat down to supper, and the twelve apostles with him. And he said to them: 'I have heartily longed to eat this Passover with you before I suffer.'"[8] That it was the last time he did not learn afterwards; he knew beforehand that it is the last time.[9] Yet he did not have the heart to initiate the apostles entirely into how close the danger is, that it is this very night, and what the danger is, that it is the most ignominious death, and how inevitable it is. He who alone bore the sin of the world,[10] he also bears here alone his frightful knowledge of what will happen there. He who struggled alone in Gethsemane,[11] alone, because the disciples slept, he is also alone here, even though he sits at supper with his only confidants. Thus what will happen this night, how it will happen, by whom it will happen, there is only one person in that little circle who knew, he who was betrayed—yes, and then one more, the betrayer, who is also present.[12] So Christ sits down to supper with the apostles, and as he takes a seat at the table he says: "I have heartily longed for this meal."

My listener, does it not seem to you that this really belongs to the Lord's Supper in a deeper sense, both intimately and exemplarily, not

---

5. See Luke 22:19–20.

6. See Luke 22:3–6.

7. Loosely quoted from the 1819 Danish edition of the New Testament in *Biblia, det er, Den Ganske Hellige Skrifts Bøger* (Kiøbenhavn: C. F. Schubart, 1819).

8. See Luke 22:14–15.

9. See Luke 22:16.

10. See John 1:29.

11. See Matthew 26:36–46; Mark 14:32–42; Luke 22:39–46; John 18:1–2.

12. See Luke 22:21; John 18:2.

merely in the way it belongs historically to the sacred account? For is it not true that heartfelt longing belongs essentially to Holy Communion? Would it not also be the most frightful contrast to the sacred account of how the institutor longed heartily for this meal, would it not be the most frightful contrast if it were possible that someone from habit, or because it was common practice, or perhaps was impelled by quite incidental circumstances, in short, if someone went to the sacred meal of the Lord's Supper without heartfelt longing! The sacred text just read is then, if I dare say so, the introductory words to the institution of the Lord's Supper, and this in turn is the true godly introduction or entrance for every individual: to come with heartfelt longing.

So let us then use the prescribed moments before the communion to speak on:

the heartfelt longing for the sacred meal
of the Lord's Supper.

It is not anything new we shall teach you, even less shall we lead you into difficult investigations by leading you outside faith; we shall merely strive to express what was stirring within you when you felt the longing to go to communion, the heartfelt longing with which you came here today.

The wind blows where it will; you sense its whistling, but nobody knows where it comes from or where it goes.[13] So also with longing, the longing for God and the eternal, the longing for our Savior and Atoner. Comprehend it you cannot, nor should you; indeed, you dare not even want to attempt it—but you should use the longing. Should the merchant be responsible if he does not use the opportune moment, should the seafarer be responsible if he does not use the favorable wind? How much more the one who does not use the opportunity of longing when it is offered. Oh, people talk piously about not squandering God's gifts, but what better and in a deeper sense should be called God's gifts than every prompting of the spirit, every tug of the soul, every fervent stirring of the heart, every holy sentiment, every devout longing, which surely are God's gifts in a far deeper sense than food and clothes,[14] not only because it is God who gives them but because God gives himself in these gifts! And yet how often a person

13. See John 3:8.
14. See Matthew 6:25–34.

squanders these gifts of God! Alas, if you could peer into the inner-most being of persons and very deeply into your own, you would sure-ly discover with dismay how God, who never leaves himself without witness,[15] lavishes these his best gifts on every human being, and how on the contrary every human being more or less squanders these gifts, perhaps throwing them away entirely. What a frightful responsibility when one day, in eternity if not before, recollections rise up accusingly against a person, recollections of the many times and the many ways in which God spoke to him in his inner being but in vain. Recollec-tions, yes, for even if the person himself has long since forgotten what was squandered so that he therefore does not remember it, God and eternity have not forgotten it, it is recalled to him and in eternity be-comes his recollection.

Now it is like that with longing. A person can ignore its call, he can turn it into a momentary impulse, into a whim that vanishes with-out a trace in the next instant, he can resist it, he can prevent its deeper formation within him, he can let it die unused like an unproductive mood. But if you receive it with gratitude as a gift from God, then it will also become a blessing to you. Oh, never let this holy long-ing therefore return empty-handed when it wants to visit you; even if it sometimes seems to you that by following it you returned empty-handed—do not believe it, it is not so, it is impossible that it can be so, it may yet become a blessing to you.

So then longing awakened in your soul. Even if it was inexpli-cable, inasmuch as it is indeed from God, who draws you in it; even if it was inexplicable, inasmuch as it is by him "who lifted up from the earth will draw all to himself" (John 12:32); even if it was inexplicable, inasmuch as it is the work of the Spirit in you—you still understood what was required of you. For truly, even though God gives every-thing, he also requires everything, requires that the person himself must do everything in order to use rightly what God gives. Oh, in the ordinary pursuits of daily life how easy it is, spiritually understood, to doze off; in the routine course of monotony, how difficult to find a break! In this respect God assisted you through the longing which he awakened in your soul. You then promised yourself and God, is it not true, that you would now also gratefully use it. You said to yourself: "Just as the longing has torn me away from what so easily entangles

15. See Acts 14:17.

a person in a spell, so by earnest thoughts I shall also come to its assistance in order to tear myself completely away from what might still hold me back. And by holy resolutions I shall strive rightly to hold on to what those earnest thoughts permit me to understand, for resolution is useful in securing oneself in what one has understood.

"What sheer vanity, after all, the earthly and the temporal are![16] And even if my life thus far has been so fortunate, so carefree, so entirely without acquaintance with a frightening or even merely sad experience, I shall now call forth those earnest thoughts. Allied with the longing for the eternal and with the holy meal before my eyes, to which no one dare come without being well prepared, I shall not be afraid of becoming earnest. For Christianity, after all, is not melancholy; on the contrary, it is so joyful that it is glad tidings to all the melancholy; only the frivolous and defiant can it make gloomy-minded. Behold, everything, everything I see is vanity and vicissitude as long as it exists, and in the end it is the prey of corruption. Therefore, when the moon rises in its splendor, with that pious man[17] I shall say to the star, 'I do not care about you; you are indeed now eclipsed'; and when the sun rises in all its grandeur and darkens the moon, I shall say to the moon, 'I do not care about you; you are indeed now eclipsed'; and when the sun goes down, I shall say, 'I thought as much, for all is vanity.'[18] And when I see the bustle of running water, I shall say, 'just keep on running, you will never fill the sea';[19] and to the wind I shall say, yes even if it tears up trees by the roots, I shall say to it, 'just keep blowing; after all, there is no meaning or thought in you, you symbol of inconstancy.'[20] Even if the loveliness of the field that charmingly captivates the eye, and even if the melodiousness of the birdsong that falls blissfully upon the ear, and even if the peace of the forest that invitingly refreshes the heart were to employ all their persuasion, I still shall not allow myself to be persuaded, shall not allow myself to be deceived, I shall remind myself that it is all illusion. And even though the stars have been ever so firmly fixed through thousands of years without changing position in the heavens, I still shall not allow myself to be deceived by this stability; I shall remind myself that some day they must fall down.[21]

16. See Ecclesiastes 1:2.
17. See Ecclesiastes 1:1.
18. See Ecclesiastes 1:5, 12:2–8.
19. See Ecclesiastes 1:7.
20. See Ecclesiastes 1:6.
21. See Matthew 24:29.

"So I shall remind myself how uncertain everything is, that a human being is cast out into the world at birth and from that moment lies upon the depth of a thousand fathoms, and every moment, yes every moment the future is for him like the darkest night. I shall remind myself that never has anyone been so fortunate that he could not indeed become unfortunate, and never anyone so unfortunate that he could not indeed become more unfortunate![22] That even if I were to succeed in having all my wishes fulfilled, in having them brought up into one building—that still no one, no one would be able to guarantee me that just at the same moment the whole building would not collapse upon me. And if I succeeded (supposing this could otherwise be called a success) in rescuing a wretched scrap of my former good fortune out of this ruin, and if I prepared my soul to be patiently content with this—that still no one, no one would be able to guarantee me that at the next moment this remnant also would not be taken from me! And if there were one or another misfortune, one or another horror, a brief or slowly torturing one, that I especially dreaded, and even if I had already become a very old man—that still no one, no one would be able to guarantee me that it would not be able to come upon me even at the last moment!

"So I shall remind myself that just as every uncertainty of the next moment is like the dark night, so in turn the explanation of every single event or incident is like a puzzle that no one has solved. That no one who would speak the truth in an eternal sense can tell me with certainty which is which, whether it would actually be more beneficial to me that all my wishes were fulfilled or that they were all denied. And even if, like a shipwrecked person, I saved myself upon a plank from certain death, and even if my dear ones gladly greeted me on the beach and marveled at my rescue—that nevertheless the wise person would be able to stand by and say, 'perhaps, perhaps it would have been better for you if you had perished in the waves,'[23] and perhaps, perhaps he is just telling the truth! I shall remind myself that the wisest person who has ever lived and the most stupid person who has ever lived get equally far when it comes to guaranteeing the next

---

22. Probably an allusion to a statement by the Athenian sage Solon to the sixth-century BCE Lydian King Croesus as reported by Herodotus. See *The Landmark Herodotus: The Histories,* ed. Robert B. Strassler, trans. Andrea L. Purvis (New York: Pantheon, 2007), Bk. 1:30–33.

23. See Plato's *Gorgias,* 511d–512b.

moment, and when it comes to explaining the slightest occurrence get equally far to a 'perhaps,' and that the more passionately someone rages against this 'perhaps,' the closer he is only to losing his mind. For no mortal has broken or pushed through; indeed, not even the prisoner who sits within walls fourteen feet thick, chained hand and foot, bolted to the wall, is so constrained as every mortal is in this clamp made from nothing, in this 'perhaps.' I shall remind myself that even if my soul were concentrated in one single wish, and even if it were concentrated in it so desperately that I would be willing to throw away the blessedness of heaven for the fulfillment of this wish—that yet no one could say for certain to me in advance whether the wish, when it was fulfilled, still would not seem empty and meaningless to me. And what then is more miserable, that the wish was not fulfilled and I retained the sad and painful idea of the—missed good fortune, or that it was fulfilled and I retained it, embittered by the certainty of how empty it was!

"So I shall bear in mind that death is the only certainty, that mocking, mocking me and all the uncertainty of earthly life, which at every instant is equally uncertain, it is equally certain at every instant; that death is no more certain for the old man than for the infant born yesterday; that whether I am overflowing with health or lying upon a sickbed, death is equally certain for me at every instant, a fact of which only earthly apathy can remain ignorant. I shall remember that no covenant, not the most tender nor the most heartfelt, is entered into between human beings without also being entered into with death, which is officially present in everything.

"And I shall remind myself that every human being is after all alone, alone in the infinite world. Yes, in good days, during calm weather when fortune smiles, it does indeed seem as if we live in association with one another. But I shall remind myself that no one can know when news might come to me, news of misfortune, misery, horror,[24] which along with the frightfulness of it would also make me alone or make it evident how alone I am, like every human being, make me alone, deserted by those nearest and dearest to me, misunderstood by my best friend, an object of anxiety that everyone avoids. I shall remind myself of the horrors which indeed no cry of alarm, no tears, no appeals averted, the horrors that have separated a lover from

24. See Job 1:13–19.

the beloved, a friend from friend, parents from children; and I shall remind myself of how a little misunderstanding, if it then went fatally wrong, sometimes was enough to separate them horribly. I shall remind myself that *humanly* speaking there is no one, no one at all to rely on, not even God in heaven. For if I truly held fast to him, I would then become his friend—oh, who has suffered more, who has been more tested in all sufferings than the pious person who was God's friend."[25]

This is how you talked with yourself; and the more you abandoned yourself to these thoughts, the more the longing for the eternal triumphed in you, the longing for communion with God through your Savior, and you said: "I heartily long for this meal. Oh, there is after all only one friend, one trustworthy friend in heaven and on earth, our Lord Jesus Christ. Alas, how many words a person employs and how many times he goes to get another person to do him a favor, and if this other person does him a favor only with some sacrifice, he who has learned to know human beings and knows how seldom favors are done when they cannot be returned, how firm he then sticks to his benefactor! But he who also for me, yes for me (for that he did the same for all others certainly ought not to diminish my gratitude, which of course is for what he has done for me), he who died for me— should I not long for communion with him! No friend has ever been able to be more than faithful *unto* death,[26] but he proved to be faithful precisely *in* death[27]—his death was indeed my salvation. And no friend can after all do more at most by his death than *save* another's life,[28] but he *gave* me life by his death; it was I who was dead, and his death gave me life.

"But *sin* is the corruption of nations and of every human being; how then could I think earnestly about life without properly bearing in mind what Christianity teaches me, that the world lies in evil![29] And even if my life so far has gone by so quietly, so peacefully, so unaffected by the evil world's attacks and persecutions, and even if it seems to me that the few people I have known are after all good and loving

25. See James 2:23.
26. See Revelation 2:10.
27. See Philippians 2:8.
28. See John 15:13.
29. See 1 John 5:19.

and kind—I shall thus bear in mind that this may well be due to the fact that neither they nor I have been led out into the kind of perilous spiritual decisions of life where the magnitude of events makes it very clear on an extraordinary scale what good or evil resides in a person. That may well be so, and therefore it is necessary for revelation to teach what the human being cannot know by himself, how deep humanity has sunk.

"So I shall remind myself of what I have heard about all the atrocities which human being has committed against human being, enemy against enemy, alas and friend against friend, about violence and murder and bloodthirstiness and bestial cruelty, about all the innocently and yet so cruelly shed blood that cries out to heaven,[30] about cunning and craftiness and deceit and faithlessness, about all those innocently and yet horribly tortured persons, as it were, whose blood, to be sure, was not shed, although they were certainly destroyed. Above all I shall remind myself how it went for the Holy One when he wandered here upon the earth, what opposition he suffered from sinners,[31] how his whole life was nothing but suffering of soul by belonging to the fallen human race, which he wanted to save and which did not want to be saved, how the living person who is cruelly chained to a corpse can suffer no more torturously than he suffered psychically by becoming embodied as a human being in the race! I shall keep in mind how he was mocked and how every person was greeted with loud applause when he could think of a new insult, how there was no longer any mention, not even a thought, of his innocence, of his holiness, how the only mitigating words spoken were the commiserating words: 'Behold, what a man!'[32]

"Suppose I had lived at the same time as that appalling scene, suppose I had been present in 'the crowd' that mocked him and spat upon him![33] Suppose I had been present in the crowd—for I dare not believe that I among a whole generation would have been one of the twelve—suppose I had been present! Well, but neither can I believe of myself that I would have been present *in order to* take part in the mockery. But suppose now that the bystanders noticed that I

30. See Genesis 4:10.
31. See Hebrews 12:3.
32. See John 19:5.
33. See Matthew 26:67–68, 27:27–31; Luke 22:63–65; Mark 14:65, 15:16–20.

was not taking part—oh, I see already those savage glances, see the attack in an instant turn against me, I already hear the cry, 'he too is a Galilean,[34] a follower, kill him, or let him take part in the mockery, in the people's cause!' Merciful God! Alas, how many are there indeed in each generation who have courage to stick to a conviction when it involves the danger of insult, when it involves life and death, and when, moreover, the decisive situation of danger stands so frightfully unexpected over one! And I, who after all was not a believer, a follower, where would I find strength to venture, or how would it be possible for me to have become a believer at that instant, so that the decisive situation of danger might help me just as wondrously, even though in another way, as it helped the robber on the cross;[35] and if I was not changed in this way, where would I get courage to venture this for one who, after all, was a stranger to me! Merciful God, then I certainly would have participated in the mockery—in order to save my life, I would have cried out 'His blood be on me'[36]—in order to save my life; yes, it is true, it would have been in order to save my life! Oh, I know well enough that the priest talks differently; when he speaks he describes the terrible blindness of those contemporaries— but we who are present at his sermon, we are not that sort of people. Perhaps the priest does not have the heart to speak severely to us— yes, and if I were the priest, I would not speak differently either, I would not dare say to any other person that he would have acted in this way; there are things which one person does not dare say to another. Oh, but to myself I certainly dare say and unfortunately I must say it: it would not have gone any better for me than the multitude of people!"

This is how you talked with yourself. And the more you abandoned yourself to these thoughts, the more the longing for communion with him, the Holy One, triumphed in you, and you said to yourself: "I heartily long for this meal; away from this evil world where sin exercises dominion, I will long for communion with him! Away from it; but that certainly does not happen so easily. I can wish myself away from the world's vanity and corruption, and even if a wish cannot do it, the heartfelt longing for the eternal is still able to lead me away; for

34. See Luke 22:59 with reference to the disciple Peter.
35. See Luke 23:39–43.
36. See Matthew 27:25.

in the longing itself the eternal *is,* just as God *is* in the sorrow that is *for* him.[37] But sin has a power of its own to resist; it has an outstanding balance to exact, a debt it wants to have paid by the sinner before it relinquishes him. And sin knows how to stand up for its rights; truly, it does not let itself be deceived by loose words, not even if people entirely abolished the word 'sin' and put 'weakness' in its place, not even if, strictly speaking, a person became guilty only in weakness. But for this reason I long all the more heartily to renew my communion with him who has also made satisfaction for my sin, has made satisfaction for my every slightest actual sin, but also for the one that perhaps lurks deepest in my soul without my being aware of it and that could still possibly break out when I am led into the most frightful decisive situation. For were those Jews presumably greater criminals than other people? Oh no, but that they were contemporary with the Holy One made their crime so infinitely more terrible."

I long heartily for this meal, for this meal that is in remembrance of Him.[38] But when such a person with heartfelt longing has partaken of the Lord's Supper, is the longing then quenched, must the longing then decrease as one goes away? Look, if you have a dear one who is dead, then it will certainly also happen, for example, that time after time the longing to remember him will awaken in you. Then you perhaps go to his grave; and just as he now lies sunk in the bosom of the earth, so you sink your soul into the recollection of him. The longing is thereby somewhat satisfied. Life again exercises its power over you; and even if you continue faithfully to remember the departed one and often long for him, it still cannot mean that you should live more and more out of life in order to live in the grave with the dead, so that the longing for him increased every time you visited his grave. You yourself will certainly admit that if this happened to a person, then however much we honor his faithfulness to the departed one, there would still be something abnormal in his grief. No, you understand that your paths are essentially divided, that you belong to life and to the claims that life has upon you. You understand that the longing must not increase with the years, so that you become more and more a co-tenant of the grave. Oh, but the longing for communion with your Savior and Atoner, that indeed is

37. See 2 Corinthians 7:9–10.
38. See 1 Corinthians 11:24–25.

exactly what must increase every time you remember him. He is not a dead person but one who is living; yes, you must indeed truly live in and together with him, he must indeed be and become your life, so that you do not live yourself, no longer live yourself, but Christ lives in you.[39] Therefore, just as heartfelt longing belongs to worthy remembrance, so it is in turn characteristic of heartfelt longing that the longing is increased through remembrance, so only the one went worthily to communion[40] who went there with heartfelt longing and left there with increased heartfelt longing.

39. See Galatians 2:20.
40. See 1 Corinthians 11:27–29.

[2]

Matthew 11:28

Prayer

Father in Heaven! Just as the congregation's intercessory prayer usually asks you to console all those who are sick and sorrowful, so at this hour it asks that you will give those who labor and are heavy laden rest for their souls. And yet, this is no intercession; who would dare think himself so healthy that he should only pray for others. Alas, no, everyone prays for himself, that you will give him rest for his soul. So, O God, may you give rest for the soul to each one individually whom you see laboring heavy laden in the consciousness of sin!

Matthew 11:28: Come here to me all who labor and are heavy laden![1] and I will give you rest.

"Come here, all you who labor and are heavy laden." What a strange invitation. For ordinarily when people are gathered for pleasure or for working together, they no doubt say to the strong and cheerful: "Come here, take part with us; combine your efforts with ours." But about the troubled person they say: "No, we do not want to have him with us; he only spoils the enjoyment and delays the work." Yes, the troubled person understands very well without it being said to him, and thus perhaps many a troubled person stands apart and alone, will not participate with others lest he spoil their enjoyment or delay the work. But this invitation to *all* those who labor and are heavy laden still must indeed apply to him since it applies to all who are troubled; how dare any troubled person say here: "No, the invitation does not concern me!"

---

1. Exclamation mark added by Kierkegaard.

"All those who labor and are heavy laden," all of them, no one is excluded, not a single one. Alas, what manifold diversity is denoted by these words. Those who *labor*![2] For not only does the one labor who works by the sweat of the brow for the daily bread,[3] not only does the one labor who endures the day's heat and toil in a lowly job;[4] oh, the one who struggles with heavy thoughts also labors; the one who out of concern bears the care of one or many also labors; the one who is immersed in doubt also labors, just as the swimmer is said to labor. Those who are *heavy laden*! For not only is the one heavy laden who visibly carries a heavy burden, who visibly is in difficult circumstances, but also the one is indeed heavy laden whose burden no one sees, who perhaps even labors to hide it; and not only is the one heavy laden before whom there perhaps lies a long life in privation, in pain, in troubled recollection, but also the one for whom, alas, there seems to be no future.

But how could this discourse ever be finished if it were to mention all these differences, and even if it tried to do that, it would perhaps misguide instead of guide, would distractingly draw attention to the differences instead of concentrating the mind on the one thing needful.[5] For even if the differences are ever so many, is it really the intention of the gospel that there should be a small remnant or a greater number of persons left over who may be called the fortunate ones, exempt from labor and trouble? When it invites all those who labor and are heavy laden, is it the intention of the gospel that there are still some to whom this invitation does not apply because they are actually healthy and do not need healing?[6] This is indeed the way we usually talk. For if you see a happy circle of children and there is one sick child to whom a kind person says, "come to me, my child; we will play together," then he is indeed implying that this child is sick but also that the others are actually healthy. Now might the gospel be speaking in the same way, or should we speak so foolishly about the gospel? For if such were the case, then the gospel certainly would not pertain to everyone, then it certainly would not proclaim the equality

---

2. See SKS 10:280, line 2 for correction of the missing punctuation mark in the first edition.
3. See Genesis 3:19.
4. See Matthew 20:12.
5. See Luke 10:41–42.
6. See Matthew 9:12; Mark 2:17.

of all human beings but on the contrary would posit a distinction, excluding the cheerful, just as the human invitation usually excludes the troubled. See, that is why the invitation is to be understood differently; it invites everyone. The gospel will not be an escape, consolation, and alleviation for a few troubled people; no, it applies to all those who labor and are heavy laden, that is, it applies to everyone and *requires* of every person that he shall know what it is to labor and be heavy laden. Even if, for example, you were the most fortunate of persons, alas, so that you were even envied by many, the gospel still applies just as much to you and requires that you labor and be heavy laden. Or if you were not in this way the most fortunate, the exceptionally favored person, yet you lived in happy contentment with your dearest wishes being fulfilled without need, the gospel still applies just as much to you with the invitation's requirement. And if you were in earthly need and poverty, you still are not for that reason the only one about whom the gospel speaks. Yes, even if you were so wretched that you had become like a proverb,[7] you still are not for that reason the only one about whom the gospel speaks.

The invitation, then, will not be taken in vain temporally; it therefore contains *a requirement,* it requires that the invitee labor and be heavy laden in a deeper sense. For there is a godly sorrow;[8] it pertains to nothing earthly or temporal, not your external conditions, not your future; it is for God. The one who bears this sorrow quietly, humbly in his heart—he labors. And there is a heavy burden; no worldly power can lay it upon your shoulders, but neither can any human being take it away any more than you yourself can: it is the guilt and the consciousness of guilt, or even heavier, sin and the consciousness of sin. The one who bears this burden, alas, he is heavy laden, grievously heavy laden, but yet also heavy laden precisely in the way the gospel's invitation requires. And there is a concern, a deep, an eternal concern; it does not pertain to externals, not your fortunes, those past or future; it pertains to your actions, alas, and it pertains precisely to those which a person would prefer to have forgotten, for it pertains to those actions, hidden or disclosed, by which you committed an offense against God or against another human being. This concern is repentance; whoever sighs repentantly, yes, he labors heavy laden. No

7. See Deuteronomy 28:37; 1 Kings 9:7.
8. See 2 Corinthians 7:9–10.

one, no one else labors heavy laden in this way, and yet it is precisely this that the gospel's invitation requires.

But just as the gospel requires something through its invitation, *so also it announces the promise: "I will give you rest for your soul."*[9] Rest! That is what the exhausted laborer, the weary wanderer wishes; and the sailor who is tossed about by the sea seeks rest; and the weary old man longs for rest; and the sick person who lies restlessly on the bed and finds no alleviating position, he craves rest; and the doubter who finds no foothold on the sea of thoughts, he craves rest. Oh, but only the penitent properly understands what it is to pray for rest for the soul, rest in the only thought in which there is rest for a penitent, that there is forgiveness; rest in the only utterance that can reassure a penitent, that he is forgiven; rest on the only ground that can support a penitent, that satisfaction has been made.

But this indeed the gospel also promises, that he shall find rest for his soul. And it is indeed in response to this invitation that you have come here at this hour, attentive listener. And even if it cannot be given in such a way as to be decided forever with this one time so you would never again need to go to this holy place in order to seek rest—yet rest is promised for your soul. You are on the way, and God's house is the resting place where you seek rest for your soul; but even if you come again to seek this rest, it is still certain that it is the same rest in which one day, when your last moment has come, you shall seek rest for your soul for the last time. For whether you have come today to seek rest in your youthful years or at an advanced age—oh, when your final hour comes and in the hour of death you are abandoned and alone, then you will crave as the last thing in the world to which you will no longer belong, you will crave what you crave today.

This was the promise of the invitation. But who now is the *Inviter*! For it would indeed be a frightfully confusing discourse if the invitation, "come here," was heard in the world but it was not stated where one should go. Therefore, if there were no Inviter, or if forgetfulness and doubt had taken the Inviter away, what then would be the use in continuing to obey the words of the invitation, as it would indeed be impossible to follow the invitation, since it would be impossible to find the place. But you, my listener, certainly know who the Inviter is,

9. See Matthew 11:29.

and you have accepted the invitation in order to attach yourself more firmly to him. See, he spreads his arms[10] and says: "Come here, come here to me all you who labor and are heavy laden." See, he opens his arms, in which all of us can indeed rest equally secure and equally blessed, for it was only in our Savior's earthly life that John lay his breast next to him.[11] How you come here now, how you can now be said to labor heavy laden, whether you offended in much or in little, whether the guilt is old and—yet no, it is not forgotten, oh no, but old and often repented, or it is fresh and no mitigating recollection has eased it—oh, with him you will indeed find rest for your soul. I do not know what troubles you in particular, my listener; perhaps I could neither understand your sorrow nor know how to speak with insight about it. Oh, but you do not go to any human being; from having confessed in secret[12] before God you go to him the merciful Inviter, he who knows all human sorrow, he who himself was tried in everything, yet without sin.[13] He was also acquainted with earthly need, he who hungered in the desert,[14] he who thirsted upon the cross;[15] he was also acquainted with poverty, he who had nowhere he could lay his head;[16] his soul has also been sorrowful unto death;[17] yes, he has experienced all human sorrow more grievously than any human being, he who at the bitter end was abandoned by God[18]—when he bore all the sin of the world.[19] And he is indeed not only your spiritual advisor but also your savior; he understands not only all your sorrow better than you yourself understand it, oh, but he wants precisely to take the burden from you and to give you rest for your soul. It is hard—yes, it is true—it is hard not to be understood; but what help would it be to you, after all, if there were someone who could entirely understand your sorrow but could not take it away from you, could entirely understand your strife but could not give you rest!

10. A reference to the statue of Christ by the Danish sculptor Bertel Thorvaldsen (1770–1844) that overlooks the altar in Our Lady's Church in Copenhagen, where Kierkegaard worshipped and took communion.

11. See John 13:23.

12. See Matthew 6:6.

13. See Hebrews 4:15.

14. See Matthew 4:1–2; Mark 1:12–13; Luke 4:1-2.

15. See John 19:28.

16. See Matthew 8:20.

17. See Matthew 26:38; Mark 14:34.

18. See Psalm 22:1; Matthew 27:46; Mark 15:34.

19. See John 1:29.

So there was then an invitation: "Come here all you who labor and are heavy laden"; and the invitation contained a requirement, that the invitee labor heavy laden in the consciousness of sin; and there is the trustworthy Inviter, he who still stands by his word yonder and invites all. God grant that the one who seeks may also find;[20] that the one who seeks the right thing may also find the one thing needful; that the one who seeks the right place may also find rest for the soul. For it is no doubt a restful position when you kneel at the foot of the altar, but God grant that this indeed may truly be only a faint intimation of your soul's finding rest in God through the consciousness of the forgiveness of sins.

20. See Matthew 7:7–8.

[3]

John 10:27

Prayer

Father in Heaven! Your grace and mercy change not with the changing of the times,[1] age not with the course of the years, as if you, like a human being, were more gracious on one day than on another, more gracious on the first day than on the last. Your grace remains unchanged, just as you are unchanged, the same, eternally young, new with every new day—for indeed every day you say "this very day."[2] Oh, but if a person pays attention to this phrase, is moved by it, and with pious resolve says earnestly to himself "this very day"—then for him this means that he precisely desires to be changed on this day, precisely desires that this day might be truly significant for him above other days, significant by renewed strengthening in the good he once chose or perhaps even significant by choosing the good. It is your grace and mercy unchangeably to say every day "this very day,"[3] but your mercy and time of grace would be forfeited if a human being so unchangeably were to say from day to day "this very day." You are surely the one who gives the time of grace "this very day," but the human being is the one who must seize the time of grace "this very day." This is the way we talk with you, O God; there is a linguistic difference between us, and yet we strive to understand you and to make ourselves intelligible to you, and you are not ashamed to be called our God.[4] What is the eternal expression of your unchanged grace and mercy when you say it, O God, that same phrase is the strongest expression of the deepest

1. See James 1:17.
2. See Luke 23:43; Hebrews 3:7, 13, 15, 4:7.
3. See Lamentations 3:22–23.
4. See Hebrews 11:16.

change and decision when a human being repeats it rightly understood—yes, as if everything would be lost if the change and decision
did not happen this very day. So grant then to those who are assem-
bled here today, those who, without any external summons, therefore
all the more inwardly, have resolved even today to seek reconciliation
with you in the confession of sin, grant them that this day may be
a true blessing for them, that they may have heard the voice of him
whom you sent to the world,[5] the voice of the Good Shepherd,[6] that he
may know them and that they may follow him.

John 10:27: My Sheep hear my voice, and I know them, and they follow me.

When the congregation gathers in the Lord's house on holy days, God
himself has indeed so commanded and prescribed it. Today, however,
is no holy day; and yet a small group has gathered here in the sanctuary, thus not because it is prescribed for all (since it is prescribed
for no one), but because each single individual of those present must
especially have felt a need, although in different ways, to come here
precisely today. For today is no holy day, today everyone normally
goes to his field, to his business, to his work; only these single individuals come to the Lord's house today. So the single individual, then,
left his home to come here. When on a holy day the one who is himself
going to church meets a passer-by, he naturally assumes then that this
passer-by is probably going to church too, for on a holy day, even if it
is far from always being the case, the passer-by is someone who is going to church. But the one who, impelled by an inner need, comes here
today, I wonder, would it occur to anyone who met him in passing that
he was going to God's house? Should then this visit to God's house for
that reason be less solemn? It seems to me that this secretiveness must,
if possible, make it even more inward. Openly before everyone's eyes
and yet secretly, the single individual came to church today secretly or
by the secret path, for no one knew his path except God; it occurred
to no passer-by that you were going to God's house, which not even
you yourself say, for you say that you are going to Holy Communion,
as if this were even more inward and solemn than going to church.

5. See John 3:17, 10:36, 17:18.
6. See John 10:1–18.

You did not expect, as on a holy day, that the passer-by was going by the same path and with the same thoughts; therefore you went secretly among the many people, like a stranger. You did not expect to see the same resolve expressed in the faces of those passing by; therefore you kept your eyes to yourself, did not greet them solemnly as on a feast-day. No, the passer-by did not exist at all for you; with downcast eyes you fled here, as it were, secretively. Nor was it your intention merely to worship, to praise, to thank God as on festival days, when you therefore could not wish to be alone; your intention is to seek the forgiveness of sins—so you must wish to be alone. How quiet and how solemn it is now! On a holy day everything outside is also quiet; the customary work is at a standstill; even the one who does not visit God's house still notices that it is a holy day. Today, however, is no holy day. The noise of life's daily activity outside is barely audible within these vaulted arches, where precisely for that reason the sacred stillness is all the greater. For the stillness that civil authority can order temporally is after all not godly stillness; but this stillness, while the world makes noise, is precisely the godly stillness. So it was not your duty to come here today, it was a need within you; it was no external summons that determined you, you yourself must have resolved it inwardly. No one could blame you for not coming, it is your own free choice to come; you did not do it because the others were doing it, for the others, after all, went precisely on this very day each to his field, to his business, to his labor[7]—but you went to God's house, to the Lord's altar.

And with that you have specifically expressed that you count yourself among those who would belong to Christ, those described in the sacred text just read, which was taken from the gospel where Christ compares himself to the good shepherd and the true believers to sheep. About these a threefold statement is made: they hear his (Christ's) voice; he (Christ) knows them; they follow him (Christ).

They hear his voice. And today it is especially, is simply and solely *his* voice that is to be heard. Everything else done here is just for concentrating the mind's attention on this, that it is *his* voice which is to be heard. There is no preaching today. A confessional address is not a sermon; it does not want to instruct you or impress upon you the old familiar doctrines; it only wants to give you pause on the way to the altar, in order that you through the speaker's voice may confess by your-

---

7. See Matthew 22:5.

self before God in secret. For you will not learn from a confessional address what it means to confess; it would also be too late, but through it you confess before God. There is no preaching today. What we say here in the prescribed short moment is again no sermon; and when we have said Amen, the divine service is not essentially over as usual but then the essential begins. Our discourse therefore merely wants to give you pause for a moment on the way to the altar; for today the divine service does not center as usual on the pulpit but on the altar. And at the altar what is essential above all is to hear *his* voice. It is quite true that a sermon should also witness to him, proclaim his word and his teaching; but for all that, a sermon is still not *his* voice. At the altar, however, it is *his* voice that you must hear. If another human being said to you what is said at the altar, if all people were to unite in saying it to you—if you do not hear *his* voice, then you go in vain to Holy Communion. When there at the altar every word by the Lord's servant is spoken exactly as it is handed down from the fathers;[8] when you listen carefully to every word, so that not the least thing escapes you, not a jot—if you do not hear *his* voice, that it is he who says it, then you go in vain to Holy Communion. If you faithfully appropriate every word that is said; if you earnestly resolve to take it to heart and to order your life in conformity with it—if you do not hear *his* voice, then you go in vain to Holy Communion. It must be *his* voice you hear when he says, "come here all you who labor and are heavy laden," therefore his voice that invites you. And it must be his voice you hear when he says, "this is my body."[9] For at the altar there is no speaking about him; *there* he himself is personally present, it is he who speaks—if not, then you are not at the altar. In a physical sense one can just point to the altar and say, "there it is"; but spiritually understood it is still really only *there* if you hear *his* voice *there*.

He knows them. That is, he does not know those who do not hear his voice, and neither are those he does not know his own. For it is not with him as with a human being, who can very well have a friend and a follower without being aware of it, without knowing him. But the one Christ does not know is not his own either, for Christ is omniscient—he knows them, and he knows each one individually. The sacrifice he made was not for human beings in general, nor did he want to save human beings in general—and it cannot be done in that way

8. See 1 Corinthians 11:23.
9. See Matthew 26:26; Mark 14:22; Luke 22:19; John 6:51–58.

either. No, he sacrificed himself in order to save each one individually. Should he then not know each one individually? For should not one know the person for whom one has sacrificed one's life![10]

When the congregation gathers in great numbers on festival days, he knows them as well; and those whom he does not know are not his own. Yet on such an occasion someone might easily deceive himself, as if he were the single individual hidden in the crowd. At the altar, however, no matter how many are gathered there, yes even if everyone is gathered at the altar, there is no crowd at the altar. He himself is personally present, and he knows those who are his own. He knows you, whoever you are, whether known by many or unknown by all, if you are his own, he knows you. Oh, what earnestness of eternity to be known by him; oh, what blessed consolation to be known by him. Yes, even if you fled to the extreme limits of the world, he knows you; even if you hid in the abyss, he knows you[11]—but there is certainly no reason to flee, no reason to seek a hiding place, for the blessedness is precisely that he knows you. Yet no third person can know whether he knows you; that you must know with him and with yourself—but if he does not know you, then neither are you his own. Behold, the sun rises over the earth every morning with the dawning day; its rays penetrate everywhere to every point, there is no place so remote that it does not also illuminatingly penetrate there. Yet it makes no distinction in its acquaintance with the earth, it shines equally everywhere and knows every place. But he, humankind's eternal sun, his acquaintance with humanity also penetrates like rays of light everywhere to every human being; but he makes a distinction. For there are also those he does not know, those to whom he will say, "I do not know you, I never knew you,"[12] those to whom he will say this even though they still claim that they know him! If you went up to the Lord's altar and took part in the sacred act, if you could prove ever so certainly that you had been to Holy Communion, if the Lord's servant testifies on your behalf that he has handed the bread and wine to you individually, just as to each of the others—if *he* does not know you, then you still went in vain to communion. For physically one can point to the altar and say, "see, there it is," but spiritually understood the altar is only *there* if you are *known* by him *there*.

10. See John 10:14–15.
11. See Psalm 139.
12. See Matthew 7:22–23; Luke 13:25–27.

They follow him. For you do not and shall not remain at the altar. You return again to your business, to your work, to the joy that perhaps awaits you, or alas, to the sorrow—for today all such things you have put aside, but if you are *his own,* then you follow him. And when you follow him, you do indeed leave the altar when you go away from there, but then it is as if the altar followed you, for where he is, there is the altar—and when you follow him, he accompanies you. Oh, what earnestness of eternity, that wherever you go, whatever you do, he accompanies you; oh, what blessed consolation, that he accompanies you; oh, what marvelous congruity, that the earnestness of eternity is also the most blessed consolation! The altar certainly stays put; therefore you go to the altar. But it is still only the altar if *he* is present *there*—thus where he is, there is the altar. He himself says "when you are offering your gift at the altar and you remember there that someone has something against you, then first go and be reconciled with your enemy, and then come and offer your gift."[13] Oh, which offering do you think is dearest to him, the offering you bring by reconciling with your enemy, thus by offering God your anger—or the gift you could offer at the altar! But if the offering of reconciliation is dearest to God, to Christ, then the altar is certainly also *there* where the most acceptable offering is brought. Abel sacrificed upon the altar, but Cain did not, for God had regard for Abel's offering—therefore it was an altar; but he did not have regard for Cain's offering.[14] Oh, do not forget that where he is, there the altar is, that his altar is neither on Moriah nor on Gerizim,[15] or any visible *there,* but that it is there where he is. If that were not the case, then you would have to remain at the altar, take up residence there, never budge from the spot, but such superstition is not Christianity. Today is no holy day, today there is divine service on a workday—oh, but a Christian's life is divine service every day! It is not then as if everything were therewith decided by someone going to communion on rare occasions; no, the task is, on leaving the altar still to remain at the altar. Today everything else, as we said, was merely to concentrate the mind's attention on the altar. But now when you

---

13. See Matthew 5:23–24.

14. See Genesis 4:3–5.

15. See John 4:21. Mount Moriah, where the testing of Abraham by God took place (Genesis 22:1–19), became the site of Solomon's temple in Jerusalem (2 Chronicles 3:1); Mount Gerizim, near Shechem, was the holy mount of the Samaritans, who erected a temple there that was later destroyed and never rebuilt.

depart from there, remember that the matter is not finished with that; oh no, with that the cause has just begun, the good cause, or as scripture says, the good work in you which God who began it will complete on the day of our Lord Jesus Christ.[16] No doubt you perhaps devoutly could call this day today, if what God will give you really has meaning for you, a day of Jesus Christ; but there is still only one day that is properly called the day of Jesus Christ. The day today, however, will soon be over. God grant that one day when it is long since vanished and forgotten—the blessing of this day, recollected many, many times, may still be a fresh memory for you, so that the remembrance of the blessing may be a blessing to you.

> Pass on, O day, that never more
> My eyes here in time will see,
> Fall asleep in the shade of night!
> I proceed to the kingdom of heaven
> My God to see eternally,
> On that my faith is built.[17]

---

16. See Philippians 1:6.

17. A verse from Thomas Kingo, *Psalmer og aandelige Sange af Thomas Kingo,* ed. P. A. Fenger (Kiøbenhavn, 1827), no. 184 (ASKB, no. 203).

[4]

1 Corinthians 11:23

Prayer

Remind, O Jesus, oft my heart
Of your distress, anguish, and need
Remind me of your soul's pain.[1]

Yes, you our Lord and Savior, not even in this respect do we dare put trust in our own strength, as if we were able by ourselves to evoke deeply enough or constantly to hold fast your memory, we who would so much rather dwell on the joyful than on the sorrowful, we who all desire good days, the peace and security of happy times, we who certainly wish to remain in a deeper sense ignorant of horrors lest, as we foolishly think, they might make our happy life gloomy and serious, oh, or as it seems to us, our unhappy life still more gloomy and serious. Therefore we pray to you, you who are indeed the one we want to remember, we pray to you that you yourself will remind us about that. Oh what a strange language a human being speaks when he must talk with you; it is indeed as if it had been rendered unfit for use when it has to describe our relation to you or yours to us. Is this even a remembrance when the one who is to be recollected must himself remind the one recollecting! Humanly speaking, only the high and mighty person who has so many and such important things to think about talks this way, saying to the lowly person: "You yourself must remind me to remember you." Alas, and we say the same thing to you, you the Savior and Atoner

---

1. Ove Malling, "Mind, O Jesu, tidt mit Hjerte," in *Evangelisk-christelig Psalmebog til Brug ved Kirke-og Huus-Andagt* (Kiøbenhavn, 1847), no. 147 (ASKB, no. 197).

of the world. Alas, and when we say it to you, this same thing is precisely the expression of our lowliness, our nothingness in comparison with you, you who with God are exalted above all heavens.[2] We
pray that you yourself will remind us of your suffering and death,
remind us often, at our work, in our joy and in our sorrow, of the
night in which you were betrayed. We beseech you for this and we
thank you when you remind us; we also thank you in this way, as
those who are now gathered here today, by going up to your altar in
order to renew communion with you.

1 Corinthians 11:23: . . . the Lord Jesus on the night when he was betrayed.

On the night when he was betrayed. Let it now become nothing but
night round about you, for this indeed belongs with the holy act. You
who are gathered here in order to participate in the supper that was
instituted that night in remembrance of our Lord Jesus Christ, you
yourselves have surely asked him to place his suffering and death quite
vividly before your eyes.[3] Oh, there are those who perhaps pray that
it might be granted them to see what kings and princes vainly desired to see,[4] one of his days of glory. Do not regret your choice, for
truly that person has chosen the better part[5] who first and foremost
prays that the appalling scene might stand vividly before him—on the
night when he was betrayed. It was in this way, humanly speaking,
that he has now come down in the world. He whom at one time the
people would have proclaimed king;[6] he whom later the high priests
did not dare lay hands upon because all the people were attached to
him;[7] he who by his mighty works had collected numerous crowds
around him;[8] he before whose authority as teacher all had bowed,[9]
the Pharisees defiantly but constrained,[10] the people gladly and ex-
pectantly—he is now as if thrust outside the world, he sits apart in a

---

2. See Philippians 2:9; Hebrews 7:26.
3. See Galatians 3:1.
4. See Luke 10:24.
5. See Luke 10:42.
6. See John 6:15.
7. See Matthew 21:45–46, 26:5; Mark 14:2; Luke 19:47–48, 20:19.
8. See Luke 19:36–38; John 6:2.
9. See Matthew 7:28–29.
10. See John 7:32, 45–52.

room with the twelve.[11] But the die is cast; his fate is decided by decree of the Father and the high priests.[12] When he rises from the table to go out into the night, he also goes to meet his death; then begins the scene of horror for which everything is in readiness, then he must once more experience the past in repetition of the horror, in a certain sense ending appallingly with the beginning: he shall be hailed as king, but in mockery;[13] he shall actually wear the purple robe,[14] but as an insult; he shall collect an even greater number of people around him, but the high priests will no longer be afraid to lay hands on him but rather will surely be compelled to restrain the hands of the people so it can appear as if he—is condemned to death.[15] It was, after all, a legal proceeding; he was indeed arrested "as one arrests a thief"[16] and "crucified as a criminal!"[17] Thus his life was one of retrogression instead of progression, the opposite of what the human mentality naturally thinks and desires. For temporally a person ascends from step to step in honor and prestige and power, ever more and more people approving his cause until he who was continually in the majority, at last admired by all, stands on the top step. But he [Christ] inversely descended from step to step, and yet he ascended; and the truth must suffer in this way—or be singled out for distinction in the world, as sure as he was the truth.[18] At first it seemed to please everyone, but the more obvious it gradually became, the more definite and clear, the more decisive, the more the masks of illusions fell off, the more others continually fell away[19]—at last he stands alone. But he does not stop even there; now he ascends from step to step through all the marks of abasement until he is finally crucified. Finally, yet the end did not take very long, for from the instant the scene of horror began on the night he was betrayed, the decisive moment is present with sudden speed, as when the storm darkens heaven and earth in the twinkling of an eye. This night is the limit; and then what a change! And yet in a certain sense everything is the same. The place is the same, it is the same high

---

11. See Matthew 26:17–19; Luke 22:7–13; Mark 14:12–16.
12. See Matthew 26:57–68.
13. See Matthew 27:27–31.
14. See John 19:2; Matthew 27:28.
15. See Matthew 27:20–26; John 19:6–7, 13–16.
16. See Matthew 26:55; Luke 22:52.
17. See Luke 23:33.
18. See John 14:6.
19. See John 6:66.

priests, the same governor, the people are the same—yes, and he is also the same. When on one occasion they wanted to proclaim him king, he then *fled*,[20] and when they come armed to arrest him, he then goes *to meet* the guard and says "whom do you seek?"[21] To be sure, he once greeted Judas as an apostle with a kiss, neither does he deny Judas the kiss with which he surely knows he will betray him[22]—is he then not the same!

O my listener, just as a person perhaps sometimes has a day or a night he might wish out of his life, the human race might wish this night out of its history! For if it was dark,[23] at the midnight hour, when he was born, the night in which he was betrayed was even darker! The human race might wish this night out of its history, yes and every single individual might wish it out of the history of the race. For this event is indeed not finished and long since past; Christ's suffering we must not and dare not recall as we recall those glorious ones who suffered an innocent death, about which we say, "it is now long since past." His innocent death is not past, even though the cup of suffering is empty,[24] not a bygone event, although it is past, not a past event over and done with, although it was eighteen hundred years ago, has not become that even if it was eighteen hundred years ago. To be sure, he did not die a natural death on a sickbed; nor did he come to the end of his days by accident; nor was it some individuals who attacked and killed him; nor was it that generation which crucified him—it was *the human race,* and presumably we do indeed belong to it if we are human beings at all; and in this way we are presumably present if we are human beings at all. Consequently we dare not wash our hands—at least we cannot do it except as Pilate could do it;[25] consequently we are not spectators and observers at a past event, we are indeed accomplices in a present event. Therefore we do not presumptuously delude ourselves in a poetical fashion that it is sympathy which is required of us—it is indeed his blood which is also required of us,[26] who belong to the human race. Oh, even the follower who resembled him most, who did not, as desired by superstition, bear his wounds on his body

20. See John 6:15.
21. See John 18:4.
22. See Matthew 26:47–50; Mark 14:43–45.
23. See Luke 2:8.
24. See Matthew 26:39, 42; John 18:11.
25. See Matthew 27:24.
26. See 2 Samuel 1:16; Ezekiel 3:18, 20; Matthew 27:25; Acts 5:28.

but whose life was also a retrogression instead of progression, who also, according to the Christian order of rank, ascended from step to step, derided, insulted, persecuted, crucified[27]—even he, when he is reminded of that night and it is quite present to him in thought, even he is indeed present as an accomplice! And when the congregation, every time these words are spoken, "our Lord Jesus Christ on the night when he was betrayed," anxiously but fervently closes around him as if to ward off the treason, as if to promise fidelity to him, even if everybody else deserted him[28]—yet no one dares forget that on that night he was along as an accomplice, no one dares forget that pitiful prototype which he hardly resembles otherwise, the Apostle Peter.[29] Alas, even if we human beings are of the truth,[30] we are still alongside *"the Truth"* when we must go along with the person who is "the Truth," when "the Truth" is the criterion: we are still like children alongside a giant; in the moment of decision we still remain—accomplices.

On the night when he was betrayed. What crime has more likeness to that night than an act of treason; oh, and what crime is more unlike love than an act of treason, alas, and most of all when it happens by a kiss! To be sure, Judas is the traitor, but basically they are all traitors, except Judas is the only one who does it for the sake of money.[31] Judas betrays him to the high priests, and the high priests betray him to the people, and the people to Pilate; and Pilate betrays him to death out of fear of the emperor,[32] and the disciples, who flee in the night, and Peter, who denies him in the court, do the same out of fear of people.[33] This was the end, oh, just as when the last spark goes out—then everything is dark. In the whole human race there is not one person, not a single one, who will have anything to do with *him*—and he is *the Truth*! Oh, and if you think that you would surely never have done this, you would never have laid hands on him or taken part in the derision—but betray him, that you would have done: you would have fled or you would have prudently stayed home, would have kept yourself

27. Presumably St. Francis of Assisi (1182–1226), who, according to Christian tradition, bore the stigmata, or wounds of Christ, upon his body. See also JP 1:288; JP 2:1839.

28. Se Mark 14:27.

29. See Matthew 26:69–75; Mark 14:66–72; Luke 22:54–62; John 18:25–27.

30. See John 18:37.

31. See Matthew 26:14–15.

32. See John 19:12–16.

33. See Matthew 26:56, 69–75; Mark 14:50; Luke 22:54–62.

out of it, letting your servant report to you what happened there. Alas, but to betray is the most painful blow you can inflict upon love; there is no suffering, not even the most excruciating physical suffering, in which love winces so soulfully as in being betrayed, for there is nothing so blessed to love as faithfulness!

Oh, that this happened is enough for me nevermore to be happy in the same way as the frivolous and worldly natural human being is, as the inexperienced youth is, as the innocent child is. I do not need to see more, that is, if anything else more terrible has happened in the world, anything that can terrify the heart more, for there may well be something that can terrify the senses more. Nor is there a need for anything terrible to happen to me—this is enough for me: I have seen *"Love"* betrayed, and I have understood something about myself, that I am also a human being and to be a human being is to be a sinful human being. For all that, I have not become misanthropic, least of all a hater of other people; but I will never forget this sight or what I have understood about myself. The one whom the race crucified was the Atoner;[34] precisely for that reason I feel, as someone belonging to the human race, a need for an atoner—never has the need for an atoner been clearer than when the human race crucified the Atoner. From this instant I no longer trust myself; I will not let myself be deceived, as if I were better because I was not tried like those contemporaries. No, anxious about myself as I have become, I will seek my refuge in him, the Crucified One. To him I will pray that he will save me from evil and save me from myself. Only when saved by him and with him, when he holds me fast, do I know that I shall not betray him. The anxiety that wants to frighten me away from him, so that I too could betray him, is precisely what will attach me to him;[35] then I dare hope that I shall hold fast to him—how could I not dare hope this when that which would frighten me away is precisely what binds me to him! I will not and I cannot do it, for he moves me irresistibly; I will not shut myself up inside myself with this anxiety about myself without having confidence in him; I will not shut myself up inside myself with this anxiety or with this consciousness of guilt that I too have betrayed him—I would rather, as a guilty one, belong to him redeemed. Oh, when he wandered about in Judea, he moved many by his beneficial

34. See. Ephesians 1:7; Colossians 1:13–14; Hebrews 9:11–12.
35. See CA, 118–62.

miracles; but nailed to the cross he performs an even greater miracle, he performs the miracle of love, so that without doing anything—by suffering he moves every person who has a heart!

He was betrayed—but he was Love: *on the night when he was betrayed,* he instituted the meal of love! Always the same! Those who crucified him, for them he prayed;[36] and on the night when he was betrayed he uses the occasion (oh, the infinite depth of love that finds precisely this moment opportune!), he uses the occasion to institute the meal of reconciliation. Truly, he did not come into the world to be served without reciprocating![37] A woman anoints his head; in return she is remembered through all the centuries![38] Yes, he reciprocates for what people do against him! People crucify him—in return his death upon the cross is the sacrifice of atonement for the sin of the world, also for this, that people crucified him! People betray him—in return he institutes the meal of reconciliation for all! If Peter had not denied him, then there would still have been one person who would not like every other individual in the human race wholly have needed reconciliation. But now they all betrayed him, and thus all also need to participate in the meal of reconciliation.

See, everything is now ready;[39] blessed is the one who for his part is now also ready! See, he is waiting there at his holy table—so do this then in remembrance of him, and for blessing to yourself!

36. See Luke 23:34.
37. See Matthew 20:28; Mark 10:45.
38. See Matthew 26:6–13.
39. See Luke 14:17.

[5]

2 Timothy 2:12–13

Prayer

Lord Jesus Christ, you who loved us first,[1] you who until the last loved those whom you had loved from the beginning,[2] you who continue until the end of time to love everyone who wants to belong to you: Your faithfulness cannot deny itself—alas, only when a person denies you can he as it were compel you, you loving one, also to deny him. So may this be our consolation when we must indict ourselves for whatever offenses we have committed and whatever we have left undone, our weakness in temptations, our slow progress in the good, that is, our unfaithfulness to you, to whom we once in early youth[3] and repeatedly thereafter promised faithfulness—may it be our consolation that even if we are unfaithful, you still remain faithful, you cannot deny yourself.

2 Timothy 2:12–13: . . . if we deny [him], he will also deny us; if we are faithless, he still remains faithful; he cannot deny himself.

It might seem that the sacred text just read contains a contradiction, and if this were the case it might not only seem but would be strange even to call attention to such a text. However, this is by no means so. The contradiction would presumably lie in the fact that in the one clause it says that if we deny him, he will also deny us, and in the other that he cannot deny himself. But should there be no difference,

---

1. See 1 John 4:19.
2. See John 13:1.
3. Probably an allusion to the ritual of confirmation in the Evangelical Lutheran Church of Denmark.

then, between denying him and being unfaithful to him? It is certainly clear enough that the one who denies him is also unfaithful to him, for no one can deny him without having belonged to him; but it does not follow from this that everyone who is unfaithful to him therefore also denies him. If this is so, then there is no contradiction. One is the strict clause, the other the lenient; indeed, here is the law and the gospel, but both clauses are the truth. Nor is there any duplexity in the text, but it is the one and same word of truth that separates people, just as the eternal truth, both in time and in eternity, separates them in good and evil.[4] Just as it is reported in the sacred scriptures that only when the Pharisees had gone away did Christ first begin to speak intimately with the disciples,[5] so the first clause removes, sends away, alas, as to the left side those who deny him, whom he also will deny;[6] the latter clause, the lenient word of consolation, is spoken as to those on the right side.[7] For he who bade his disciples not to cast their pearls to swine,[8] his love, even if it wants to save everyone, is not a weakness that whiningly needs those who should be saved but is compassion towards everyone who needs to be saved.

But you who are gathered here to participate in the holy meal certainly have not denied him, or in any case you are indeed gathered to confess him, or by being gathered today with the intention of doing that, you do indeed confess him. Even though it can therefore be profitable that the strict word be brought to mind and heard with that to which it inseparably belongs, so that we might not at any moment separate what God has joined together in Christ,[9] neither add anything nor subtract anything,[10] do not take from the leniency the strictness that is in it, from the gospel the law that is in it, from the salvation the perdition that is in it—the latter word nevertheless lends itself so preeminently well to being dwelt upon today. We let the terrifying thought pass by, not as something irrelevant to us; oh no, no one is saved in such a way; as long as one lives, it would still be possible that one could be lost. As long as there is life there is hope[11]—but as long as

4. See Matthew 25:31–33.

5. See Matthew 15:1–20; Mark 4:10–11, 7:1–23.

6. See Matthew 25:41.

7. See Matthew 25:34.

8. See Matthew 7:6.

9. See Matthew 19:6; Mark 10:9.

10. See Revelation 22:18–19.

11. See N. F. S. Grundtvig, *Danske Ordsprog og Mundheld* (Kiøbenhavn, 1845), no. 1022, p. 38 (ASKB, no. 1549).

there is life there is surely also the possibility of danger, consequently of fear; and so just as long there must also be fear and trembling.[12] We let the terrifying thought pass by; but then we hope to God that we dare let it pass by and cross over while we console ourselves by the gospel's lenient word.

He still remains faithful. Thus in your relation to him you have one less concern, or rather one more blessedness than any human being can ever possibly have in relation to another human being. Humanly speaking, in the relation between two persons, each individual always has a dual concern; he has the one for himself, that he will now remain faithful; oh, but in addition he has the one whether the other will also remain faithful. But he, Jesus Christ, remains faithful. In this relationship, therefore, the peace and blessedness of eternity is whole; you have only one concern, the self-concern that you remain faithful to Christ—for he remains eternally faithful. Oh, there is surely no perfectly happy love except that with which a person loves God;[13] and no perfectly blessed faithfulness except that with which a person attaches himself to Christ. Everything, unconditionally everything that God does is serviceable to you; you need not fear that anything could escape him that would be to your benefit, for only he knows what is to your benefit. You need not fear that you would not be able to make yourself understood by him, for he understands you completely, far better than you understand yourself. You have only to rejoice (oh, the infinite felicity of love!) in his love—to be silent and to give thanks! To be silent and to give thanks; yes, for when you are silent, then you understand him, and best when you are completely silent; and when you give thanks, then he understands you, and best when you give thanks always.[14] So happy is a person's love with which he loves God.

But it is also like that with the faithfulness that attaches itself to Christ. Oh, in the heart of every person's soul there dwells a secret anxiety that even the one whom he trusted most could become unfaithful to him. No merely human love can entirely drive out this anxiety,[15] which can very well remain hidden and unnoticed in the friendly security of a happy life-relationship but which at times can inexplicably stir within and is immediately at hand when the storms

---

12. See Philippians 2:12; see also FT.
13. See 1 John 2:5, 4:17–18.
14. See Ephesians 5:20; 1 Thessalonians 5:18.
15. See 1 John 4:18.

of life begin. There is only one person whose faithfulness can drive out this anxiety, and that is Jesus Christ. He remains faithful; yes, even if every other faithfulness were to fail, he still remains faithful, every day of your life, whatever happens to you; he remains faithful to you in death; he then meets you again in the hereafter as a trusty friend. In your relation to him you have no concern at all about his unfaithfulness; this anxiety, that when you had given yourself completely, had your whole life in him, that he could then be unfaithful to you, it shall never, indeed it dare never visit you. No, strengthened by eternity's certainty of his faithfulness, you have increased strength (and this, to be sure, is also his gift) to devote everything so that you may be faithful to him. You must not be engaged in two places at once, as is generally the case with troubled thoughts. By his faithfulness, which he himself eternally guarantees, he wants to make you unconcerned, set your mind at ease, support you, but certainly also by such faithfulness exhort you to remain faithful to him.

If we are faithless—he still remains faithful. Thus in your relation to him you have one less concern, or rather one more blessedness than any human being can ever possibly have in relation to another human being. For if in the relationship between two persons one became unfaithful but repented his unfaithfulness and returned—alas, perhaps his unfaithfulness might have had power to change the other person so that he could not bring himself to forgive him. But he, our Lord Jesus Christ, remains faithful to himself. It would certainly be presumptuous and blasphemous if someone were to think that by his unfaithfulness he has power to change him [Christ], power to make him less loving than he was, that is, than he is. But it would also be ungodly if someone were able to take his faithfulness in vain. You shall not take the Lord your God's name in vain;[16] oh, but also be mindful that you do not take Christ's faithfulness in vain lest you turn it into a punishment upon yourself; for just as his unchanged faithfulness is forgiveness for the penitent, is it not likewise a curse upon the one who impotently rebels and hardens himself!

Even if we are unfaithful, he still remains faithful. When he walked here on earth, no sufferer came to him without finding help, no troubled person left disconsolately from him, not even a sick person touched the hem of his garment without being healed (Mark

16. See Exodus 20:7.

6:56)—but if someone had come to him the seventieth time and had asked him for forgiveness for his unfaithfulness, do you believe he would have become weary, even if it had been seven times seventy![17] No, heaven will become weary of supporting the stars and cast them away before he becomes weary of forgiving and thrusts a penitent away from himself. Oh blessed thought, that there still exists one faithful, one trusty friend, that he is that; blessed thought, that is, if a person dare entertain this thought at all; all the more blessed, there-fore, that he is the trusty friend of the penitent, the unfaithful! Alas, perfect faithfulness is never found in the world—provided that any-one is justified in seeking it in others; but perfect faithfulness in return for unfaithfulness, that is found only with our heavenly teacher and friend—and surely we all need to seek that. Yes, if it were possible that you, our Teacher and Savior, could one day become weary of our perpetual assurances of faithfulness, these assurances that certainly are not hypocritical or fabricated but yet to you must often or always sound so feeble, so childish; if you could one day have the heart to test our faithfulness quite in earnest; if you were to throw us out into the current, as the teacher commonly does with the pupil, and say "now I will not help you at all but merely test your faithfulness"—then we would indeed be instantly lost!

Oh, when it comes to characterizing our relation to the deity, this human language is certainly second-rate and half-true; even when we speak in the strongest terms of God testing us, the talk is still mean-ingless if the implied meaning is not understood: that basically God is holding on to us. When we see a mother playing the game with her child that the child is walking alone although the mother is holding it behind—and we then see this child's indescribable, jubilant face, its self-satisfied look and its manly demeanor, then we smile at the child because we see the context. But when we ourselves speak about our relation to God, then it must be in dead earnest about our walking alone, then we speak in the strongest terms about God laying his hand heavily upon us, as if he actually did not use his hand for anything else at all, or as if he did not have two hands, so that even at such a mo-ment he was holding on to us with one hand. And so we truly do not presume to demand of you, our Teacher and Savior, that you should put our faithfulness to you to a test, for we know very well that at the

17. See Matthew 18:21–22.

moment of testing you yourself must hold on to us; that is, we know very well that we are *basically* unfaithful and that at every moment it is *basically* you who is holding on to us.

Attentive listeners, you are gathered here today to renew your pledge of faithfulness, but by what path are you reaching your decision? It is indeed through confession. Is this not a detour? Why do you not go straight to the altar? Oh, even if it were not prescribed by sacred tradition, would not you yourself still feel the need to go by this path to the altar! The confession certainly does not want to burden you with the guilt of unfaithfulness; on the contrary, through confession it wants to help you to discard the burden. The confession will not force you to confess; on the contrary, it will relieve you through confession; in the confessional there is no one who accuses you if you do not accuse yourself. My listeners, you have all heard what the priest said in the confessional; but what you said to yourself about yourself, that no one knows except you who said it and God who heard it. Yet it is certainly not the priest who will go to the altar, but it is you. Nor was it the priest who confessed; he did not even hear your confession, but it was you who confessed before God in secret. This God has heard, but what God has heard, he whom you seek at the altar has also heard; if you have forgotten something, alas, or if you have deceptively forgotten something, God knows it and he whom you seek at the altar also knows it. Far be it from us even to try with the discourse, as it were, to examine ourselves with regard to whatever unfaithfulness a person may well have to reproach himself for, which can indeed be extremely diverse. No, according to the sacred tradition of our church, this is entrusted to your honesty toward God. But nevertheless bear in mind that even if the interval since you last renewed your fellowship with your Savior belonged to what a person humanly might call a better time—alas, how much unfaithfulness may not there still be in your relation with him to whom you certainly did not promise faithfulness in some particular, not in this or that, but unconditionally in everything! Alas, who knows himself! Is it not exactly this to which earnest and honest self-examination[18] leads as its last and truest result, this humble confession: "Who knows his errors? From my hidden faults cleanse thou me" (Psalm 19:12). And when a person examines his relation to Christ, who then is the human being that entirely knows

18. See 2 Corinthians 13:5.

his unfaithfulness, who the human being that dares think that in self-examination there could not again be unfaithfulness! In this respect, therefore, you do not find rest. So rest then; so seek rest then for your soul[19] in the blessed consolation that even if we are faithless, he is still faithful.

He cannot deny himself. No, he cannot shut himself up inside himself with his love, he who out of love sacrificed himself for the world. But the one who shuts himself up inside himself and refuses to have anything to do with others, he indeed denies himself. He denies being at home when you come to look for him; and if you did get to see him after all, you would seek in vain to grasp his hand, for he draws it back and denies himself; you would seek in vain to catch his eye, because he averts it and denies himself; you would seek in vain an expression of sympathy in his countenance, for he withdraws and denies himself. But he, our Lord Jesus Christ, he does not deny himself, he cannot deny himself. See, for that reason he spreads out his arms there at the altar,[20] he opens his arms to all; you see it in him, he does not deny himself. He does not deny himself; and neither does he deny what you ask him for when you now renew your pledge of faithfulness to him. He is the same; he was and he remains faithful to you.

19. See Matthew 11:29.
20. Another reference to the statue of Christ by the Danish sculptor Bertel Thorvaldsen that overlooks the altar in Our Lady's Church in Copenhagen where Kierkegaard worshipped and took communion.

[6]

1 John 3:20

Prayer

Great are you, O God; although we only know you as in a mystery and as in a mirror,[1] we still adore your greatness in wonder—how much more must we one day extol it when we learn to know it more fully! When I stand under the dome of heaven surrounded by the wonder of creation, then moved and with adoration I praise your greatness, you who easily support the stars eternally and concern yourself in a fatherly manner with the sparrow.[2] But when we are gathered here in your holy house, then we are also surrounded on all sides by what in a deeper sense reminds us of your greatness. For great are you, the Creator and Sustainer of the world; but when you, O God, forgave the world's sin and reconciled yourself with the fallen human race, ah, then you were indeed even greater in your incomprehensible compassion! How could we then not believingly praise and thank and worship you here in your holy house, where everything reminds us of this, especially those who are gathered today to receive the forgiveness of sins and to appropriate anew reconciliation with you in Christ!

1 John 3:20: . . . even if our hearts condemn us, God is greater than our hearts.

Even if our hearts condemn us. When the Pharisees and the scribes had brought a woman who was caught in open sin to Christ in the temple in order to accuse her,[3] and when after that, shamed by his

---

1. See 1 Corinthians 13:12.
2. See Matthew 6:26, 10:29; Luke 12:6.
3. See John 8:3–11.

answer, they were all gone away, Christ said to her, "has no one condemned you?" but she said, "no one, Lord." Thus there was no one
who condemned her. So also here in this sanctuary there is no one
who condemns you; if your heart condemns you, you yourself alone
must know. No one else dare know it, for this other person after all is
also concerned today with his own heart, whether it condemns him.
Whether your heart condemns you is no one else's business, for this
other person also has only to do with his own heart, its accusing or
its acquitting thoughts. How you were affected when these words, "if
our hearts condemn us," were just read is no one else's business, for
this other person also devoutly applies everything to himself, thinks
only about how he felt, whether the words surprised him like a sudden
thought, or he heard, alas, what he had said to himself, or he heard
what he thought did not apply to him after all. For a heart may very
well accuse itself, but from this it still does not follow that it must
condemn itself; and we of course do not teach melancholy exaggera-
tion any more than we teach wanton indulgence. But when it comes to
speaking about the text just read, how could one find better listeners
than upon a day such as this and such as those who have come here
today, not from the distractions of the world but from the concentration of the confessional, where each one individually has made an accounting to God, each one individually has let his heart be the accuser,
which it is also best qualified to be since it is the confidant, and which
it had better be in a timely fashion lest one day it might appallingly become that against the person's own will. Yet there certainly is a difference between guilt and guilt; there is a difference between owing five
hundred pieces of silver and only fifty;[4] the one person can have far, far
more to reproach himself for than another; there may also be one who
must say to himself that his heart condemns him. Perhaps there may
also be such a person present here or perhaps there is no such person
present here—but certainly all of us still need consolation. And I suppose it cannot be disheartening to anyone that the word of consolation
is so rich in compassion that it includes everyone; this certainly cannot be disheartening to anyone, even if his heart does not condemn
him. Yet it is essentially the same consolation we all need, we whose
hearts do not acquit us: God's greatness, that he is greater than our
hearts.

4. See Luke 7:41.

*God's greatness is in forgiving, in showing mercy, and in this his
greatness he is greater than the heart that condemns itself.* Look, it is
this greatness of God that should be especially spoken of in the holy
places, for here we know God in a different way, more intimately, if
one dare say so, from another side than outside, where he is certainly
manifest, is known in his works,[5] whereas here he is known as he has
revealed himself, as he wants to be known by the Christian. The signs
by which God's greatness in nature is known everyone can *wonder-
ingly* see, or rather, there is really no sign, for the works themselves are
signs; for example, everyone can see the rainbow and must wonder
when he sees it. But the sign of God's greatness in showing mercy is
only *for faith;* this sign is indeed the sacrament. God's greatness in
nature is *manifest;* but God's greatness in showing mercy is a *mystery,*
which must be believed. Precisely because it is not directly apparent to
everyone, precisely for that reason it is called and is the *revealed.* God's
greatness in nature immediately awakens *astonishment* and then *adoration;* God's greatness in showing mercy is first an occasion *for offense*
and then *for faith.* When God had created everything, he looked and
lo "it was all very good";[6] and appended, as it were, to every one of his
works is: *praise, thank, worship the creator.* But appended to his greatness in showing mercy is: *blessed is the one who is not offended.*[7]

All our discourse about God is naturally human discourse. However much we endeavor to preclude misunderstanding by revoking in
turn what we say—if we do not wish to be wholly silent, we must after
all use human criteria when we human beings speak about God. What
now is true human greatness? Surely it is greatness of heart. Properly speaking, we do not say that a person who has much power and
dominion is great, yes, even if there lived or had lived a king whose
sovereignty was over the whole earth—however hasty our amazement
is to immediately call him great—the more profound person does not
allow himself to be disturbed by appearance. And on the other hand,
even if it were the lowliest person who has ever lived—when you witness his action in the moment of decision, seeing that he truly acts no-
bly, magnanimously forgives his enemies with his whole heart, makes
the utmost sacrifice in self-denial, or when you witness the inner for-
bearance with which he lovingly endures evil from year to year—then

5. See Romans 1:19–20.
6. See Genesis 1:31.
7. See Matthew 11:6.

you say, "he is indeed great, he is truly great." So greatness of heart is the true human greatness, but greatness of heart is precisely to conquer oneself in love.

Now then, when we, human beings as we are, want to form a conception of God's greatness, we must think about true human greatness, consequently about love and about the love that forgives and shows mercy. But what does this signify? Might the meaning be that we really want to compare God with a human being, even if this human being were the noblest, the purest, the most forgiving, the most loving person who has ever lived? Far from it. Neither does the apostle speak this way. He does not say that God is greater than the most loving human being but that he is greater than the heart that condemns itself. In this way God and the human being thus resemble each other only inversely. Not by the steps of direct resemblance—great, greater, greatest—do you arrive at the possibility of comparison; it is only possible inversely. Nor is it by more and more lifting up his head that a human being draws increasingly close to God, but inversely by casting himself down deeper and deeper in worship. The contrite heart[8] that condemns itself cannot have, seeks in vain to find, an expression strong enough to describe its guilt, its wretchedness, its defilement—even greater is God in showing mercy! What a strange comparison! All human purity, all human mercy is not good enough for comparison; but a penitent heart that condemns itself—with this God's greatness is compared in showing mercy, except that it is even greater: as deep as this heart can lower itself, and yet never deep enough, so infinitely exalted, or infinitely more exalted is God's greatness in showing mercy! See, language seemingly bursts and breaks in order to characterize God's greatness in showing mercy; thought sought a comparison in vain, then finally found it in what, humanly speaking, is no comparison, the contrition of a penitent heart—even greater is God's mercy. A penitent heart, when in contrition it condemns itself; yes, this heart allowed itself no rest, not for a single instant, it found no hiding place where it could flee from itself, it found no possible excuse, found it a new, the most appalling excuse to seek an excuse, it found no, no relief, even the most compassionate word that the most compassionate inwardness was able to think up sounded to this heart, which dared not and would not let itself be consoled, like a new condemnation upon it—so

8. See Psalm 51:17.

infinite is God's greatness in showing mercy, or it is even greater. It limps, this comparison—that is what a human being always does after striving with God.[9] This comparison is no doubt far-fetched, for it was found by piously rejecting all human likeness. If a human being dare not make for himself any image of God,[10] then assuredly he does not imagine that human nature could be a direct comparison. Let no one be in too great a hurry in seeking, let no one be precipitate in wanting to have found a comparison for God's greatness in showing mercy. Every mouth shall be stopped,[11] every person shall beat his breast[12]—for there is only one comparison, after all, that is tolerable, an anxious heart that condemns itself.

But God is greater than this heart! So be consoled after all. Perhaps you learned earlier from experience how hard it is for such a heart to be summoned to appear before the judgment of Pharisees and scribes, or to arrive at the misunderstanding that only knows how to tear it to pieces even more, or at the pettiness that simultaneously disquiets the heart even more, you who so greatly needed someone who was great. God in heaven is greater; he is not greater than the Pharisees and the scribes, nor greater than misunderstanding and pettiness, nor greater than the person who nevertheless knew how to speak a soothing word to you, with whom you found some solace because he was not petty-minded, would not put you down even more but raise you up—God is not greater than he (a hopeless comparison!), no, God is greater than your own heart! Oh, whether it was a sickness of the soul that so darkened your mind every night that finally in deadly anxiety, brought almost to madness by the conception of God's holiness, you thought you must condemn yourself; whether it was something frightful that so weighed upon your conscience that your heart condemned itself—God is greater! If you will not believe, if you dare not believe without seeing a sign,[13] now it is indeed offered. He who came to the world and died, he died also for you, also for you. He did not die for human beings as such in general; oh, just the opposite, if he died for anyone in particular, then it was certainly for the one, not for the ninety-nine[14]—alas, and you are certainly too wretched to be

9. See Genesis 32:24–32.
10. See Exodus 20:4.
11. See Romans 3:19.
12. See Luke 18:13.
13. See Matthew 12:38–39; John 2:23, 4:48, 6:30.
14. See Matthew 18:12–14; Luke 15:3–7.

included at random in the round number; the weight of wretchedness and guilt fell upon you so frightfully that you are counted out.
And he who died for you when you were a stranger to him,[15] would
he abandon his own![16] If God so loved the world that he gave his only
begotten son[17] in order that no one would be lost, how could he then
not save those who were dearly bought![18] Oh, do not torture yourself;
if it is the anxieties of melancholy that ensnare you, then God knows
everything—and he is great! And if it is the heavy load of guilt that
rests upon you—he, who of himself, in what did not arise in any human heart,[19] took compassion on the world, he is great! Do not torture yourself; remember that woman, that there was no one who condemned her, and consider that the same thing can also be expressed
in another way: Christ was present. Precisely because he was present,
there was no one who condemned her. He rescued her from the condemnation of the Pharisees and the scribes; they went away ashamed
because Christ was present—there was no one who condemned her.
Thus Christ alone remained with her—but there was no one who condemned her. Precisely this, that he alone remained with her, signifies
in a far deeper sense that there is no one who condemns her. It would
have helped her but little that the Pharisees and the scribes went away;
after all, they could come back again with condemnation. But the *Savior* remained alone with her—therefore there was no one who condemned her. Alas, there is only one guilt that God cannot forgive, that
of not willing to believe in his greatness!

For he is greater than the heart that condemns itself. But on the
other hand there is nothing about his being greater than the worldly,
frivolous, poor heart that foolishly counts on God's imagined greatness in forgiving. No, God is and can be just as scrupulous as he is
great and can be great in showing mercy. In this way God's nature always unites opposites, just as in that miracle of the five small loaves.[20]
The people had nothing to eat—by a miracle superabundance was
provided there; but behold, after that Christ enjoins them carefully
to gather up every leftover crumb. How divine! For one person can
be wasteful, another thrifty; but if there were a human being who by

15. See Romans 5:10.
16. See John 13:1; 1 Corinthians 6:19–20.
17. See John 3:16.
18. See 1 Corinthians 6:20; 7:23.
19. See 1 Corinthians 2:9.
20. See Matthew 14:13–21; Mark 6:30–44; Luke 9:12–17; John 6:1–14.

a miracle could at any moment—divinely procure a superabundance, do you not believe that he—humanly would have left a few crumbs, do you not believe that he—divinely would have gathered up the crumbs! So also with God's greatness in showing mercy; a human being scarcely has a mere idea of how scrupulous God can be. Let us not deceive ourselves, lie to ourselves and, what is the same thing, diminish God's greatness by wanting to make ourselves better than we are, less guilty, or by designating our guilt with more frivolous names, for with that we diminish God's greatness, which is in forgiving. But neither let us madly want to sin even more in order to make the forgiveness even greater;[21] for God is just as great in being scrupulous.

And so let us then here in your holy house praise your greatness, O God, you who incomprehensibly showed your mercy and reconciled the world to yourself.[22] Behold, the stars outside proclaim your majesty,[23] and the perfection of everything your greatness; but in here it is the imperfect, it is the sinners who praise your even greater greatness! The supper of remembrance is once again prepared, so may you then be remembered and thanked in advance for your greatness in showing mercy.

---

21. See Romans 3:7–8; 6:1–2.
22. See 2 Corinthians 5:19.
23. See Psalm 148:3.

[7]

Luke 24:51

Prayer

You who came down from Heaven to bring blessing to the fallen human race; you who walked here on earth in poverty and lowliness, misunderstood, betrayed, insulted, condemned—but blessing; you who while blessing was parted from your own that you may ascend again to heaven:[1] Our Savior and Atoner, bless also those who are gathered here today their participation in this holy meal in remembrance of you. Oh, there is always something missing in every meal if the blessing is lacking—what after all would the holy Lord's Supper be without your blessing; it would not exist at all, for it is indeed the meal of blessing.[2]

Luke 24:51: And it happened, as he blessed them, he was parted from them.

"As he blessed them, he was parted from them." These words contain the account of his ascension. He was parted from them "and was carried up into heaven" (Luke 24:51); "a cloud took him out of their sight" (Acts 1:9), but the blessing remained behind. They saw him no more, but they were sensible of the blessing; "they were gazing up toward heaven" (Acts 1:10), for he was parted from them while *blessing*. But he is always parted from his own in this way, while blessing them; oh, and he always comes to his own in this way, blessing them; and he is always with his own in this way, blessing them. He is not parted from

---

1. See John 3:13.
2. See Luke 24:30.

anyone in any other way unless that person himself bears the terrible responsibility for it. Just as that progenitor of the Jewish people said when he wrestled with God, "I will not let you go unless you bless me,"[3] so he says, as it were, "I shall not leave you without blessing you, and every time you meet with me again, I shall not part from you without blessing you." When those who are gathered here today to meet with him return home from this meeting, people wish for them a blessing, for they are convinced that when they were parted from him or when he was parted from them, he blessed them.

Attentive listener, whatever a person is going to undertake, whether the work is great and significant or lowly and insignificant, he is able to do nothing if God does not give his blessing. The master builder works in vain if God does not give his blessing;[4] the wise ponder in vain if God does not give his blessing; the rich accumulate abundance in vain if God does not give his blessing, for first and last it is the blessing that satisfies when you have abundance, and it is the blessing that turns poverty into abundance. But is it now also true that no work succeeds and prospers unless God blesses it? Oh, the human undertaking that succeeds even extraordinarily is often seen, although God certainly did not bless it. Yes, this is so, and therefore we must say that the one who wants merely—to have the aid of God's blessing in order that, humanly speaking, the undertaking might succeed, does not pray worthily; he does not even understand what he is asking for, or he even presumes to want God to serve him instead of him serving God. No, the blessing is the good in itself, it is the one thing needful,[5] is infinitely more glorious and more blessed than all success. What then is the blessing? The blessing is God's consent that the undertaking which a person asks God to bless may be undertaken. And what does it mean that he prays for the blessing? It means that he dedicates himself and his undertaking to serving God—regardless of whether or not, humanly speaking, it succeeds and prospers. Therefore we must say that every godly undertaking is futile if God does not bless it, for it is only a godly undertaking by God's blessing it.

No doubt every undertaking can be and ought to be a godly undertaking, but the more decisively it is a godly undertaking and the more clearly a person is conscious that it is a godly undertaking he is

3. See Genesis 32:26.
4. See Psalm 127:1.
5. See Luke 10:42.

up to, the more deeply and with greater clarity he feels the need of the blessing, that it is futile if God does not bless it. For instance, to pray is a godly undertaking, but is it not also the thought that lies closest to the one praying, that God will bless his prayer, not first of all that God will grant his request but that God will bless his prayer so that it might be or become the right prayer! What does a person pray for? For the blessing—but then, first and foremost for the blessing to pray or in order to pray. It is a godly undertaking to go to the house of the Lord; but is not this also the thought that lies closest, that it may be a blessing! What does a person seek in God's house? The blessing—but then, first and foremost that God, as it is piously phrased, will bless his entering.[6] Indeed, the clearer it becomes that it is a godly act you are up to, to the same degree the deeper the need of the blessing also becomes clear to you, for the more you become involved with God, the clearer it becomes how much less you yourself are capable of doing. If you become involved with him with your whole mind and with all your strength,[7] then it becomes quite clear that you yourself are capable of doing nothing at all, and all the more clear it becomes that you absolutely need the blessing.

But to go to communion is indeed in the strictest sense a holy act, a godly undertaking. You go to communion—it is for this holy act that you are gathered here today; you go to communion in order to meet with him for whom you long more every time you are parted from him. But if you as a human being are nothing before God, therefore altogether in need, at the altar you are, as a sinner, less than nothing in relation to the Atoner, and all the more deeply you feel the need for the blessing. At the altar you are capable of doing nothing at all. And yet precisely at the altar it is a question of making satisfaction for guilt and sin, for your guilt and your sin. The more it is required that you be able to do something, and the more this is made necessary when you are nevertheless able to do nothing, all the more clear it therefore becomes and all the more deeply you then understand that you are able to do less than nothing—but all the more clear then is the need for the blessing, or that it is everything. At the altar you are able to do nothing at all. Satisfaction is made there—but by another; the sacrifice is made—but by another; the atonement is accomplished—by

---

6. See Psalm 121:8.
7. See Deuteronomy 6:4; Mark 12:30.

the Atoner. All the more clear it therefore becomes that the blessing is everything and does everything. At the altar you are able to do less than nothing. At the altar it is you who are in the debt of sin, you who are separated from God by sin, you who are so infinitely far away,[8] you who forfeited everything, you who dared not step forward—it was another who paid the debt, another who accomplished the reconciliation, another who brought you close to God, another who suffered and died in order to restore everything, another who steps forward for you. If at the altar you want to be able to do the least thing yourself, even merely to step forward yourself, then you upset everything, prevent the atonement, make the satisfaction impossible. At the altar it holds true as was said to that ungodly person who in a storm implored heaven for deliverance, "by all means do not let God notice that you are present."[9] Everything depends upon another being present at whom God looks instead of looking at you, another whom you count on because you yourself only draw back. At the altar, therefore, he is present giving a blessing, he who while blessing was parted from his own, he to whom you are related as the infant was related to him when he blessed it,[10] he your Savior and Atoner. You cannot meet him at the altar as a co-worker as you no doubt can meet God as a co-worker in your occupation. In relation to the atonement you cannot be a co-worker of Christ, not in the remotest way. You are wholly in debt, he is wholly the satisfaction. All the more clear is it indeed that the blessing is everything. For what is the blessing? The blessing is what God does; everything God does is the blessing; the part of the work in relation to which you call yourself God's co-worker,[11] the part God does, is the blessing. But at the altar Christ is the blessing. The divine work of the atonement is Christ's work, and in relation to it the human being can do less than nothing—consequently the blessing is everything, but if the work is Christ's, then Christ is indeed the blessing.

At the altar you are able to do nothing at all, not even this, to hold fast the thought of your unworthiness, and in this to make yourself receptive to the blessing. Or would you dare, even if it were only at the

8. See Luke 18:13.

9. A statement by Bias, one of the seven Greek sages, as reported by Diogenes Laertius in *Lives of Eminent Philosophers,* 2 vols., trans. R. D. Hicks (Cambridge, Mass.: Harvard University Press, 1979–80), 1:89.

10. See Mark 10:13–16.

11. See 1 Corinthians 3:9; 2 Corinthians 6:1.

last moment as you step up to the altar, would you dare, even in relation to the thought that recognizes its own unworthiness, would you dare vouch for yourself, trust in yourself, that you would be able to keep away everything disturbing, every anxious thought of recollection, alas, that wounds from behind, every suddenly awakened mistrust that turns itself against you as if you still were not sufficiently prepared, every most fleeting delusion of self-confidence! Alas, no, you are capable of nothing at all, not even of holding your soul by yourself on the point of being conscious that you stand entirely in need of grace and the blessing. Just as another supported Moses when he prayed,[12] you must likewise be supported at the altar by the blessing on receiving the blessing; it must surround and stand by you while being communicated to you. The priest who is present at the altar is neither able to communicate the blessing to you nor to support you; only he is able to do it who is himself personally present, he who not only communicates but is the blessing at the altar. He is himself present; he blesses the bread when it is broken,[13] it is his blessing in the cup that is handed to you.[14] But it is not merely the gifts that are blessed; no, the meal itself is the blessing. You partake not only of the bread and the wine as blessed but on partaking of the bread and the wine you partake of the blessing, and this is really the meal. Only he who instituted this meal can prepare it[15]—for at the altar he is the blessing.

See, he therefore spreads out his arms yonder at the altar;[16] he bows his head toward you—blessing! In this way he is present at the altar. Then you are parted from him again or then he is parted from you again—but while blessing. God grant then that it may also become a blessing to you!

12. See Exodus 17:12.
13. See Luke 24:30.
14. See 1 Corinthians 10:16.
15. See Mark 14:12–16.
16. Another reference to the statue of Christ behind the altar at the Church of Our Lady.

PART TWO

"The High Priest"—"The Tax Collector"—"The Woman Who Was a Sinner": *Three Discourses at the Communion on Fridays* (1849)

Preface

May "that single individual, whom I with joy and gratitude call *my* reader,"[1] receive this gift. I dare say it is more blessed to give than to receive,[2] but if this is so, in one sense the giver is precisely the needy one, in need of the blessedness of giving; and if this is so, its greatest benefaction is indeed to the one who receives—and so it is after all more blessed to receive than to give.

May he receive it! What I thought I saw the first time when I sent forth the little book (see the Preface to *Two Upbuilding Discourses* 1843) that was compared and in fact could best be compared with "an insignificant little flower under the cover of the great forest,"[3] I see again "how that bird which I call *my* reader suddenly casts an eye upon it, swoops down on its wings, plucks it and takes it for himself."[4]

---

1. See the preface to "Two Upbuilding Discourses" (1843) in EUD, 5.
2. See Acts 20:35.
3. See the preface to "Two Upbuilding Discourses," 5 (translation modified).
4. Ibid. (translation modified).

Or, from another angle and with a different figure, I see again what I saw that time, how the little book "wends its way along lonely paths or solitary along the public highways . . . until it finally meets that single individual whom I call *my* reader, that single individual whom it seeks, to whom it so to speak stretches out its arms"[5]—that is, I saw and see that the little book is received by that single individual whom it seeks and who seeks it.

Early September 1849   S. K.

---

5. Ibid. (translation modified).

[8]

Hebrews 4:15

Prayer

Where should we go if not to you, Lord Jesus Christ![1] Where should the sufferer find sympathy if not in you, and where the penitent, alas, if not in you, Lord Jesus Christ!

Hebrews 4:15: For we do not have a high priest who is unable to have sympathy with our weaknesses, but one who has been tested in all things in the same way, yet without sin.

My listener, whether you yourself have been, possibly are a sufferer, or whether you have become acquainted with sufferers, perhaps with the noble motive of wanting to console, you have no doubt often heard this, which is the universal complaint of sufferers: "You do not understand me, oh, you do not understand me, you do not put yourself in my place; if you were in my place, or if you could put yourself in my place, if you could put yourself entirely in my place, and thus entirely understand me, then you would speak differently." You would speak differently; this means, according to the sufferer, that you also would perceive and understand that there is no consolation.

This then is the complaint; the sufferer almost always complains that the one who wants to console him does not put himself in his place. No doubt the sufferer is also always somewhat right, for no human being experiences exactly the same thing as another human being, and even if that were the case, it is the universal and common

---

1. See John 6:68.

limitation of every human being in particular not to be able to put himself entirely in another human being's place, even with the best intention not to be able to perceive, feel, think quite like another human being. But in another sense the sufferer is wrong insofar as he thinks that this means that there is no consolation for sufferers, for it could indeed also mean that every sufferer must try to find consolation within himself, that is, in God. It surely was not at all God's will that the one human being should be able to find complete consolation in the other; on the contrary, it is God's gracious will that every human being must seek it in him, that when the grounds of consolation which others offer become insipid to him he then turns to God, following the word of scripture: "Have salt in yourselves and be at peace with one another."[2] Oh you sufferer, and oh you who perhaps honestly and with good intentions wish to console—do not fight the futile fight with each other![3] You sympathizer, show your true sympathy by not claiming to be able to put yourself entirely in the other's place; and you sufferer, show your true discretion by not requiring the impossible of the other—there is indeed still one who can entirely put himself in your place just as in every sufferer's place: the Lord Jesus Christ.

It is about this that the sacred text just read speaks. "We do not have a high priest who is unable to have sympathy with our weaknesses," that is, we have someone who can have sympathy with our weaknesses, and further "we have one who has been tested in all things in the same way." This is exactly the condition for *being able* to have true sympathy—for the sympathy of the inexperienced and untested is a misunderstanding, most often for the sufferer a more or less troublesome and wounding misunderstanding—this is the condition, to be tested in the same way. When such is the case, then one can also entirely put oneself in the sufferer's place; and when one is tested in all things in the same way, one can then put oneself entirely in every sufferer's place. We have such a high priest who *can* have sympathy. And that he *must* have sympathy, you of course perceive that from the fact that it was out of sympathy that he was tested in all things in the same way. It was indeed sympathy that determined him to come to the world; and it was again sympathy, it was in order to be able to have true sympathy, that he, by a free decision, became tested in all things

2. See Mark 9:50.
3. See 2 Timothy 4:7.

in the same way, he who can entirely put himself and entirely puts himself in your, in my, in our place.

About that we shall speak in the prescribed brief moment.

Christ put himself entirely in your place. He was God and became a human being[4]—in this way he put himself in your place. This is indeed exactly what true sympathy certainly wants; it certainly wants to put itself entirely in the sufferer's place in order to really be able to console. But this is also what human sympathy is unable to do; only divine sympathy can do that—and God became a human being. He became a human being; and he became the human being who of all, unconditionally all, has suffered the most; no human being was ever born or ever will or can be born who must suffer as he did. Oh what security for his sympathy, oh what sympathy to give such a security! Sympathizing, he opens his arms to all sufferers; "come here," he says, "all you who suffer and are heavy laden";[5] "come here to me," he says; and he vouches for what he says, for he—this is the invitation a second time—he was unconditionally the greatest sufferer. It is already great if human sympathy ventures to suffer almost as much as the sufferer—but out of sympathy, in order to ensure the consolation, to suffer infinitely more than the sufferer, what sympathy! Human sympathy usually shrinks back, would rather remain, commiserating, on the safe beach; or if it ventures out, it is not at all willing to go as far out as where the sufferer is—but what sympathy to go farther out! You sufferer, what do you require? You require that the sympathizer shall entirely put himself in your place—and he, sympathy itself, puts himself not only entirely in your place, he came to suffer infinitely much more than you! Oh, to a sufferer this perhaps sometimes seems, discouragingly, almost so outwardly treacherous that sympathy holds back a little—but here, here sympathy is behind you in its infinitely greater suffering!

He put himself, he can put himself entirely in your place, you sufferer, whoever you are. Is it temporal and worldly worry, poverty, concern about your livelihood and what pertains to it? He too has suffered hunger and thirst and precisely in the most difficult moments of his life when he was also contending spiritually in the desert and on the cross.[6] And for daily use he possessed no more than the lily of the field and the

4. See John 1:14; Philippians 2:5–8.
5. See Matthew 11:28.
6. See Matthew 4:1–11; John 19:28–30.

bird of the air[7]—so much as that, I suppose, even the poorest possess! And he who was born in a stable, wrapped in rags, laid in a manger,[8] throughout his life he had no place where he could lay his head[9]—so much shelter, I suppose, even the homeless have! Should he not then be able to put himself entirely in your place and understand you!

Or is it a broken heart? He too once had friends, or rather, he thought once to have them, but then when the decisive moment came, they all abandoned him, yet no, not all, two remained behind, the one betrayed him, the other denied him![10] He too once had friends, or he thought once to have them; they attached themselves so closely to him, they even quarreled about who should occupy the place on his right and who on his left side,[11] until the decisive moment came and he, instead of being elevated to the throne, was raised upon the cross.[12] Then two thieves were forced against their will to occupy the empty place on his right and the empty place on his left side![13] Do you not think that he can entirely put himself in your place!

Or is it sorrow over the wickedness of the world, over what opposition you and the good must suffer, if only it is otherwise altogether certain that it truly is you who wills the good and true. Oh, in this respect, you, a human being, I suppose, would not dare to compare yourself with him; you, a sinner, I suppose, would not dare to compare yourself with him, the holy one, who experienced these sufferings first—so at most you can suffer in likeness to him—and eternally sanctified these sufferings—thus yours too, if you otherwise suffer in likeness to him—he who was despised, persecuted, insulted, mocked, spat upon, flogged, mistreated, tortured, crucified, abandoned by God and crucified amid universal jubilation.[14] Whatever you have suffered and whoever you are, do you not think that he is entirely able to put himself in your place!

Or is it sorrow over the world's sin and ungodliness, sorrow over the fact that the world lies in evil, sorrow over how deep humanity

7. See Matthew 6:26, 28–29.
8. See Luke 2:1–7.
9. See Matthew 8:20; Luke 9:58.
10. See Matthew 26:45–56.
11. See Mark 10:35–41.
12. See John 3:14.
13. See Mark 15:27; Matthew 27:38; Luke 23:32–33.
14. See Mark 9:12, 14:65, 15:19–20, 29–32; John 5:16; Luke 18:32, 22:63–65, 23:11, 39; Matthew 27:26, 29–31, 39, 41, 46.

has fallen, sorrow over the fact that gold is virtue, that power is right, that the crowd is truth, that only lies prosper and only evil prevails, that only self-love is loved, that only mediocrity is blessed, that only prudence is esteemed, that only half-measures are praised and only contemptibleness succeeds. Oh, in this respect you, a human being, I suppose, would not dare to compare your sorrow with the sorrow that was in—the Savior of the world,[15] as if he were unable to put himself entirely in your place!—And so it is with respect to every suffering.

Therefore you sufferer, whoever you are, do not despairingly shut yourself up with your sufferings, as if no one, not even he, could understand you. Do not shout impatiently about your sufferings either, as if they were so frightful that not even he was entirely able to put himself in your place. Do not have the audacity for this falsehood; bear in mind that he unconditionally and absolutely without comparison was of all sufferers the one who suffered most. For if you want to know who the greatest sufferer is, well then let me tell you. It is not the concealed cry of silent despair, and not what terrifies others, the loudness of the cry, that decides the outcome; no, just the opposite. He is unconditionally the greatest sufferer of whom it is veritably true—by the fact that he does it—that he unconditionally has no other consolation than this: to console others; for this and only this is the expression for the truth that no one can truly put himself in his place, plus that it is truth in him. And so it was with him, the Lord Jesus Christ; he was not a sufferer who sought consolation from others, still less did he find it in others, still less did he complain about not finding it in others; no, he was *the* sufferer whose only, unconditionally whose only consolation was to console others. See, here you have come to suffering's highest point, but also to suffering's limit, where everything is inverted; for he, precisely he is "the Consoler."[16] You complain that no one can put himself in your place; preoccupied day and night with this thought, it perhaps never occurs to you, I can imagine, that you should console others—and he, "the Consoler," he is the only one of whom it truly holds that no one can put himself in his place—how true, if he had complained in that way! He, "the Consoler," in whose place no one could put himself, he can entirely put himself in your place and in

15. See John 4:42.
16. See 2 Corinthians 1:3–7; 2 Thessalonians 2:16–17.

every sufferer's place. If it were true that no one at all can put himself in your place, all right then, demonstrate it; there is then only one thing left for you—become yourself the one who consoles others. This is the only evidence that can be produced for its being true that no one can put himself in your place. As long as you talk about no one being able to put himself in your place, you have not definitely made up your mind about it; otherwise you would at least be silent. But even if you were silent, as long as it does not have the effect of you taking it upon yourself to console others, you have not definitely made up your mind whether no one can put himself in your place. You merely remain sitting, then, in silent despair, again and again preoccupied with the thought that no one can put himself in your place; that is, you must firmly fix this thought at every moment; that is, it is not firmly fixed, you have not definitely made up your mind about it; that is, it is not entirely true in you. Yet neither can it be true in any human being that no one, absolutely no one can put himself in his place; for precisely he, Jesus Christ, in whose place no one either entirely or even approximately can put himself, precisely he can put himself entirely in your place.

He put himself entirely in your place; whoever you are, you who are tested in temptation and spiritual trial, he can put himself entirely in your place, "tested in all things in the same way."

As with the sufferer, so with the person who is tempted and spiritually tried, he too generally complains that whoever wants to console or counsel or caution him does not understand him, cannot entirely put himself in his place. "If you were in my place," he says, "or if you could put yourself in my place, you could understand with what terrible power temptation envelops me, you could understand how frightfully spiritual trial mocks my every effort—then you would judge differently. But you who do not feel it yourself, you can easily speak calmly about it, easily use the occasion to feel yourself superior because you did not fall into temptation, did not succumb to spiritual trial, that is, because you were neither tested in the one nor in the other. If you were in my place!"

O my friend, do not fight any futile fight that only further em-bitters life for yourself and another—there is still one who can en-tirely put himself in your place, the Lord Jesus Christ, who "because he suffered and was tempted himself is able to help those who are tempted" (Hebrews 2:18). There is one who can entirely put himself in your place, Jesus Christ, who truly learned to know every temptation by enduring every temptation.[17] If it is a concern about nourishment, and quite literally a concern about food in the strictest sense, so that starvation threatens—he too was tempted in this way; if it is a foolhardy venture that tempts—he too was tempted in this way; if it is falling away from God that tempted you—he too was tempted in this way; he can entirely put himself in your place, whoever you are. If you are tempted in solitude—so too was he, whom the evil spirit led out into solitude in order to tempt him. If you are tempted by the confusion of the world—so too was he, whose good spirit prevented him from withdrawing from the world before he had completed his work of love.[18] If you are tempted in the great moment of decision, when it is a question of renouncing everything—so too was he; or if it is in the next moment, when you are tempted to regret that you sacrificed everything—so too was he. If sinking under the possibility of danger you are tempted to wish that the actuality would soon be at hand—so too was he; if languishing you are tempted to wish for your death—so too was he. If the temptation is that of being abandoned by human beings—he too was tempted; if it is—yet no, that spiritual trial surely no human being has experienced, the spiritual trial of being abandoned by God; but he was tempted in this way. And so it was in every way.

And therefore you who are tempted, whoever you are, do not become silent in despair, as if the temptation were superhuman and no one could understand it, nor impatiently depict the magnitude of your temptation, as if even he could not entirely put himself in your place! For if you want to know what is required in order to truly be able to judge how great a temptation really is, well then let me tell you. What is required is that you have endured in the temptation. Only then do you truly come to know how great the temptation was; as long as you have not endured in it, you only know the untruth, only what the temptation, precisely in order to tempt, makes you believe about how frightful it is. To insist on truth from the temptation is asking too much. Temptation is a deceiver and liar that takes good care not to speak the truth,[19] for its power is precisely the untruth. If you want to have the truth out of it about how great it actually is, then you must see to it that you become the stronger,[20] see to it that you endure in

17. See Matthew 4:1–11.
18. See John 17:4.
19. See John 8:39–44; 2 Corinthians 11:3.
20. See Luke 11:21–22.

the temptation—then you get to know the truth, or you get the truth out of it. Therefore there is only one who truly knows quite accurately the magnitude of every temptation and can entirely put himself in the place of everyone who is tempted—he who himself was tested in all things in the same way, was tempted but endured in every temptation.

Beware, then, of more and more passionately describing and complaining about the greatness of the temptation—with every step you take along that road, you merely accuse yourself more and more. A defense of your succumbing to temptation cannot be made in this way by more and more excessively describing the greatness of the temptation, for everything you say in this respect is untruth, since you can only get to know the truth by enduring in the temptation. Perhaps another person could help you if you would let yourself be helped, another person who was tempted in the same way but endured in the temptation, for he knows the truth. But even if there is no other person who can tell you the truth, there is still one who can put himself entirely in your place, he who was tested in all things in the same way, was tempted but endured in the temptation. From him you will be able to get to know the truth, but only on the condition that he perceives that it is your honest intention to endure in temptation. And when you have endured in temptation, you will then be able to entirely understand the truth. As long as you have not endured in the temptation, you complain that no one can entirely put himself in your place—for if you have endured in the temptation, it would then indeed be all the same to you, not something to complain about if it were so that no one could put himself in your place. This complaint is an invention of the untruth that is in the temptation; and the meaning of this untruth is that if anyone could entirely understand you, then it must be someone who also succumbed to temptation, so that you two would therefore understand each other—in the untruth. Is this what it means to "understand" each other? No, here is the limit where everything is inverted—there is only one person who truly can put himself entirely in the place of everyone who is tempted—and he can do it precisely because he alone endured in every temptation. But also, oh, do not forget it, he can put himself entirely in your place.

He put himself entirely in your place, was tested in all things in the same way—**yet without sin.** So in this respect he did not put himself in your place, he cannot put himself entirely in your place, he the Holy

One,[21] how could it be possible! If the difference is infinite between God who is in heaven and you who are on earth, the difference between the Holy One and the sinner is infinitely greater.

Oh, and yet even in this respect, although in another way, he put himself entirely in your place. For if he, if the suffering and death of the Atoner is the satisfaction for your sin and guilt—if it is the satisfaction, then it indeed acts as a deputy for you, or he, the one who makes satisfaction, replaces you, suffering the punishment of sin in your place so that you may be saved, suffering death for you in your place so that you may live—did he not and does he not then put himself entirely in your place? Here it is indeed even more literally true that he puts himself entirely in your place than when we talked about it previously, where it merely signified that he could entirely understand you, while you still remain in your place and he in his place. But the satisfaction of the atonement indeed means that you step aside and that he takes your place—does he not then put himself entirely in your place?

For what is the "Atoner" but a substitute who puts himself entirely in your place and in mine; and what is the consolation of the atonement but this, that the substitute, making satisfaction, puts himself entirely in your and in my place! So when punitive justice here in the world or hereafter in the judgment seeks the place where I the sinner stand with all my guilt, with my many sins—it does not find me; I no longer stand in that place, I have left it; another stands there in my place, another who puts himself entirely in my place; I stand saved by the side of this other person, by the side of him, my Atoner, who entirely put himself in my place—for this I thank you, Lord Jesus Christ!

My listener, we have such a high priest of sympathy. Whoever you are and however you suffer, he can entirely put himself in your place. Whoever you are and however you are tempted, he can entirely put himself in your place. Whoever you are, oh sinner, as we all are, he puts himself entirely in your place! You go up now to the altar, the bread and the wine are handed to you once more, his holy body and blood, once more as an eternal pledge that by his suffering and death he put himself also in your place, so that you, saved behind him, the judgment past, may enter into life, where in turn he has prepared a place for you.[22]

21. See Mark 1:24; Luke 4:34; John 6:69; Acts 2:27, 13:35; 1 John 2:20; Revelation 3:7.
22. See John 14:2.

[9]

Luke 18:13

Prayer

Lord Jesus Christ, let your holy spirit truly enlighten and convince us of our sin, so that we, humbled with downcast eyes, acknowledge that we stand far, far off and sigh: "God be merciful to me a sinner." But then let it also happen to us by your grace according to your word about that tax collector who went up to the temple to pray: he went home to his house justified.[1]

Luke 18:13: And the tax collector stood far off and would not even lift his eyes to heaven, but beat his breast and said: God be merciful to me a sinner!

My attentive listener, the sacred text just read, as you know, is from the gospel about the Pharisee and the tax collector.[2] The Pharisee is a hypocrite who deceives himself and wants to deceive God; the tax collector is the sincere person whom God justifies. But there is also another kind of hypocrisy, hypocrites who resemble the Pharisee while having chosen the tax collector as a model, hypocrites who, according to the scripture's words about the Pharisee, "trust in themselves that they are righteous and despise others,"[3] while nevertheless shaping their character in likeness to the tax collector, sanctimoniously standing far off, unlike the Pharisee, who proudly stood by himself, sanctimoniously casting their eyes to the ground, unlike the Pharisee, who proudly turned his eyes toward heaven, sanctimoniously sighing,

1. See Luke 18:14.
2. See Luke 18:9–14.
3. See Luke 18:9.

"God be merciful to me a sinner," unlike the Pharisee, who proudly thanked God that he was righteous—hypocrites who, like the Pharisee blasphemously said in his prayer, "I thank you God that I am not like this tax collector,"[4] sanctimoniously say, "I thank you God that I am not like this Pharisee." Alas, yes, no doubt this is so. Christianity came into the world and taught humility,[5] but not everyone learned humility from Christianity; hypocrisy learned to change masks and remained the same, or rather, became even worse. Christianity came into the world and taught that you shall not proudly and vainly seek the place of honor at a banquet but shall sit at the foot[6]—and soon pride and vanity sat conceitedly at the foot of the table, the same pride and vanity, oh no, not the same, one even worse. So one might perhaps think it necessary to invert this and nearly all gospel texts, in view of the fact that hypocrisy and pride and vanity and the worldly mind may want to invert the relation. But what good would that do? Indeed, it can only be the intention of a sickly shrewdness, a conceited sagacity, to want to be so ingenious that it can prevent misuse by sagacity. No, there is only one thing that conquers and more than conquers, from the beginning has infinitely conquered all cunning, the simplicity of the gospel, which simply lets itself be deceived, as it were, and yet simply continues to be simplicity itself. And this is also the upbuilding element in the gospel's simplicity, that evil could not get power over it so as to make it sagacious, or get power over it so that it would want to be sagacious. Truly, evil has already won one and a very dangerous victory when it has induced simplicity to want to be sagacious—in order to protect itself. For simplicity is made secure, eternally secure, only by simply letting itself be deceived, however clearly it sees through the deceit.

So let us then in these prescribed brief moments simply consider the tax collector. Throughout all ages he has been described as the model of a sincere and god-fearing churchgoer. And yet it seems to me that he is even more closely related to going to communion. He who said, "God be merciful to me a sinner"—is it not as if he were now going up to the altar! He of whom it is said, "he went home to his house justified"—is it not as if he were going home from communion!

4. See Luke 18:11.
5. See Luke 14:11, 18:14.
6. See Luke 14:7–11.

The tax collector *stood far off.* What does that mean? It means to stand by yourself, alone with yourself before God—then you are far off, far away from people and far away from God, with whom you are still alone. For in relation to a human being you are closest to him when you are alone with him and farther away when others are present, but in relation to God it seems to you as if you are closer to God when several are present, and not until you are literally alone with him do you discover how far away you are. Oh, even if you are not such a sinner as the tax collector, whom human justice also judges guilty, if you are alone with yourself before God, then you also stand far away. As soon as there is anyone between you and God, you are easily deceived, as if you were not so far off. Yes, even if it were so that the person or persons before you who are between God and you are in your opinion better and more perfect than you—you are still not as far off as when you are alone before God. As soon as anyone comes between God and you, regardless of whether it is someone you consider more perfect than you or someone you consider more imperfect, you then get a fraudulent criterion, the criterion of human comparison. It is then as if how far off you are could be measured after all, and thus you are not far off.

But the Pharisee, who certainly, according to the words of scripture, "stood by himself,"[7] was he then not standing far off? Yes, if he had truly stood by himself, he would then also have stood far off, but he did not truly stand by himself. The gospel says he stood by himself and thanked God "that he was not like those other people." And when one has those other people with one, then one certainly does not stand by oneself. The Pharisee's pride consisted precisely in this, that he proudly used those other people to measure his distance from them, that before God he could not manage to get past the thought of those other people but held onto this thought in order then to stand proudly by himself—in contrast to those other people. But that is certainly not to stand by oneself, least of all is it to stand by oneself before God.

The tax collector stood far off. Being conscious of his own guilt and offense, he perhaps found it easier not to be tempted by the thought of those other people, who after all he must admit were better than he. About that, however, we shall decide nothing; but it is certain

7. See Luke 18:11.

that he had forgotten all the others. He was alone, alone with the consciousness of his guilt and offense; he had entirely forgotten that, after all, there were also many other tax collectors besides him; it was as if he were the only one. He was not alone with his guilt directly before a righteous man, he was alone before God: oh, that is to be far off. For what is further away from guilt and sin than God's holiness—and then, oneself a sinner, to be alone with it: is that not to be infinitely far off!

And he would not even lift up his eyes to heaven; that is, he cast his eyes down. Yes, well, what wonder! Even physically there is something in the infinite that overwhelms a human being, because his eye can find nothing upon which to fix itself. This effect is called dizziness—so one must shut one's eyes. And the one who, alone with his guilt and sin, knows that if he casts his eyes up he will see God's holiness and nothing else, he surely learns to cast his eyes down; or he perhaps looked up and saw God's holiness—and he cast his eyes down. He looked down, saw his wretchedness, and heavier than sleep upon exhausted eyelids, heavier than the sleep of death, the conception of God's holiness weighed down his eyes; like the exhausted person, even like the dying person, in this way he was unable to lift up his eyes.

He would not even lift up his eyes to heaven; but he—who with downcast eyes turned *in*ward, only saw *into* his own wretchedness— *did not look sideways either,* like the Pharisee, who saw "this tax collector"; for we indeed read that he thanked God that he was not like this tax collector.[8] This tax collector, yes, it is precisely the tax collector of whom we are speaking; it is of course those two men who went up to the temple to pray. The scripture does not say two men went up together to the temple to pray—indeed, neither would it have been socially fitting for the Pharisee to go up to the temple in company with a tax collector. Moreover, in the temple they seem as far as possible from being together; the Pharisee stands by himself, the tax collector stands far off—and yet, yet, the Pharisee saw the tax collector, this tax collector, but the tax collector—oh, how well in a distinctive sense you deserve to be called this tax collector!—the tax collector did not see the Pharisee. When the Pharisee got home, he knew very well that this tax collector had been in church, but this tax collector was not aware

8. See Luke 18:11.

that the Pharisee had been in church. The Pharisee proudly found satisfaction in seeing the tax collector; the tax collector humbly saw no
one, not this Pharisee either; with downcast eyes turned inward he
was in truth—before God.

And he beat his breast and said: "God be merciful to me a sinner."
O my listener, when a person is attacked by a ferocious animal in
the solitude of the desert, the cry no doubt comes of itself; and when
you fall among robbers on some out-of-the-way road, the terror itself produces the cry. So also with what is infinitely more terrible.
When you are alone, alone in the place that is more solitary than the
desert—for even in the most solitary desert it would still be possible
that another person could come there; alone in the place that is more
lonesome than the most out-of-the-way road, where it would still be
possible that another could come there; alone in particularity or as
the single individual and directly before God's holiness—then the
cry comes of itself. And when you, alone before God's holiness, have
learned that it is of no assistance to you even though your cry were to
call someone else for help, that *there,* where you are the single individual, there is literally no one else but you, that the most impossible
thing of all is that anyone else but you could be or come *there*—then
just as need has produced the prayer, the terror produces this cry,
"God be merciful to me a sinner." And the cry, the sigh is so sincere
in you—yes, how could it not be that! What hypocrisy could there
very well be in the cry of one for whom the abyss opens in distress
at sea; even though he knows that the storm mocks his feeble voice
and that the birds out there listen to him indifferently, he nevertheless cries out—to that degree the cry is genuine and true. So also
with what in an altogether different sense is infinitely more terrible,
the conception of God's holiness when a person, himself a sinner, is
alone before it—what hypocrisy could there very well be in this cry,
"God be merciful to me a sinner!" If only the danger and the terror
are real, the cry is always sincere, but furthermore, God be praised,
neither is it in vain.

The Pharisee, however, was not in danger; he stood proud, secure, and self-satisfied; from him no cry was heard. What does this
mean? It too means something entirely different: neither was he before God.

And now the conclusion. *The tax collector went home to his house
justified.*

He went home to his house justified. For what scripture says about all tax collectors and sinners, that they came *near* to Christ,[9] applies also to this tax collector: precisely by standing far off, he came near to him, while the Pharisee in presumptuous impertinence stood far, far off. Thus the picture is inverted. It begins with the Pharisee standing near, the tax collector far off; it ends with the Pharisee standing far off, the tax collector near.

He went home to his house justified. For he cast his eyes down, but the downcast eye *sees* God, and the downcast eye is the *uplifting* of the heart. Certainly no eye is as sharp-sighted as faith's, and yet faith, humanly speaking, is blind; for reason, understanding, humanly speaking, is sighted, but faith is against the understanding. The downcast eye is sighted in this way, and what the downcast eye signifies is: humility, humility is the uplifting.[10] The picture is again inverted as the two men go home from the temple. The one who was uplifted was the tax collector, and with that it ended; but the Pharisee, who began by proudly lifting up his eyes to heaven, to him God is opposed, and God's opposition is an annihilating depression. In days of old it was not as the astronomer does now, erect a building on an elevation from which he will observe the stars; formerly he dug down into the earth to find a place to observe the stars. In the relation to God no change has taken place, none takes place—to be lifted up to God is only possible by going down. No more than water changes its nature and runs uphill can a human being succeed in lifting himself up to God—by pride.

He went home to his house justified. For self-accusation is the possibility of *justification*. And the tax collector accused himself. There was no one who accused him; it was not civil justice that seized him by the breast and said, "you are a criminal"; it was not the people whom he perhaps swindled that beat him on the breast and said, "you are a swindler"—but he beat his own breast and said: "God be merciful to me a sinner." He accused himself of being a sinner before God. The picture is again inverted. The Pharisee, who far from accusing himself proudly praised himself—as he goes away, he is accused by God; he is unaware of it, but as he goes away, he accuses himself before God—the tax collector began by accusing himself. The Pharisee goes home with the new, in the strictest sense, glaring sin, with one more sin in addi-

9. See Luke 15:1.
10. See Luke 14:11, 18:14.

tion to all his earlier ones which he retained—the tax collector went home justified. Before God "to want to justify oneself"[11] is precisely to inform against oneself as guilty; but before God "to beat one's breast, saying God be merciful to me a sinner" is precisely to justify oneself, or it is indeed the condition for God's declaring you justified.

So it was with the tax collector. But now you, my listener! The similarity so obviously presents itself. From confession you go to communion. But to confess is precisely *to stand far off*; indeed, the more sincerely you confess, the farther off you stand—and it is all the more true that you then kneel at the altar, since to kneel is a symbol of standing far off, far off from the one who is in heaven, from whom the distance is then the greatest possible when you sink down to the ground kneeling—and yet at the altar you are nearest to God. To confess is precisely *to cast the eyes down,* not wanting to look up to heaven, not wanting to see anyone else; indeed, the more sincerely you confess, the more you will cast your eyes down, the less you will see anyone else— and the more truly you then kneel at the altar, since to kneel down is the even stronger expression for what it means to cast one's eyes down; for the one who merely casts his eyes down nevertheless still stands somewhat erect—and yet at the altar your heart is lifted up to God. To confess is precisely *to beat one's breast,* and, without being too upset by the thought of those particular sins, to gather all most concisely and most truly into one: *God be merciful to me a sinner.* Indeed, the more inwardly you confess, the more all your confession will end in this silent expression—beating your breast—and in this sigh—"God be merciful to me a sinner"—and the truer then your kneeling at the altar, a kneeling which expresses that you, condemning yourself, only pray for mercy—and yet at the altar is the justification.

He went home to his house justified. And you, my listener, when you return home to your house from the altar, when pious sympathy greets you with this wish, "joy and blessing," be assured that you found justification at the altar, that the visit was a joy and blessing for you. Now, before you go up to the altar, the same wish: that it may be a joy and blessing for you. Oh, the natural human being finds most satisfaction in standing erect; the one who truly learns to know God, and by learning to know God learns to know himself, finds only blessedness in falling upon his knees, worshipping when he thinks about God,

11. See Luke 10:29.

penitent when he thinks about himself. Offer him what you will, he
desires only one thing, like that woman who indeed chose—not the
best portion, oh no, how can there be here any question of comparison!—no, who chose, according to the words of scripture, the good
portion[12] when she sat down at the Savior's feet—he desires only one
thing: to kneel at his altar.

---

12. See Luke 10:38–42. The New Oxford Annotated Bible (2001) translates the
Greek την αγαθην μερίδα as "the better part," while the New English Bible (1976) has
"The part Mary chose was best." But Kierkegaard, following the Danish New Testament
of 1819, correctly translates it as "the good portion."

[10]

Luke 7:47

Prayer

Lord Jesus Christ, in order properly to be able to pray to you about everything, we pray to you about one thing: help us so that we may love you much, increase the love, inflame it, purify it. Oh, and this prayer you will hear, you who indeed surely are not—cruelly—love in such a way that you are only the object, indifferent to whether anyone loves you or not; you who indeed are not—in anger—love in such a way that you are only judgment, jealous of who loves you and who does not. Oh no, you are not like that; then you would only instill fear and anxiety, then it would be terrifying "to come to you,"[1] frightful "to abide in you,"[2] and then you would not even be the perfect love that casts out fear.[3] No, mercifully, or lovingly, or in love, you are indeed love in such a way that you yourself love forth the love that loves you, encouraging it to love you much.

Luke 7:47: Therefore, I tell you, her many sins are forgiven her, for she loved much.

My listener, you know whom the discourse is about, that it is about that woman whose name is: the woman who was a sinner.[4] "When she learned that Christ was sitting at dinner in a Pharisee's house, she fetched an alabaster jar of ointment, and she stood behind him at his feet, weeping, and began to wet his feet with tears and dried

1. See Matthew 11:28.
2. See John 6:56, 15:4.
3. See 1 John 4:18.
4. See Luke 7:36–50.

them with her hair, and kissed his feet, and anointed them with ointment."[5]

Yes, she loved much. For there are indeed contrasts that are opposed to each other in a life-and-death struggle, or for one of the contrasts it is really like the most frightful annihilation to draw near the other. It is like that when a man or a woman is a sinner—to draw near the Holy One, to become disclosed directly before him, that is, in the light of holiness. Oh, the night does not flee more terror stricken before the day that wants to annihilate it, and if there are ghosts, an apparition is not more anxiously startled when day breaks than the sinner who shrinks from the holiness that, like the day, discloses everything. Inventive in shirking excuses and equivocation and deceit and extenuation, the sinner flees as long as he can, avoids as long as he can this death march, this encounter with the light.[6] But she loved much; and what is the strongest expression for loving much? It is to hate oneself— *she went in to the Holy One.* She, a sinner! Alas, a woman; the power of the sense of shame is surely strongest in a woman, stronger than life; she would rather give up her life than give up her sense of shame. True enough, this sense of shame should certainly have kept her from, prevented her from sinning; but then in turn I suppose it is also true that when a woman comes to herself again, the sense of shame is simply all the more powerful, crushing, annihilating. Perhaps it was this that made her march to annihilation easier, that she was annihilated. And yet, humanly speaking, there could still be a question of leniency; oh, even a sinner who has truly confessed to himself or surely knows within himself that he is annihilated, he would perhaps still be lenient with himself if face to face he were to become disclosed before the Holy One; he would be lenient with himself, that is, he would surely still love himself that much. But she—is there then no leniency, none at all? No, there is no leniency!—she hated herself: she loved much.

She went in to the Holy One *in the Pharisee's house,* where the many Pharisees were gathered who would also judge her in this way: that it was vanity, disgusting vanity, especially for a woman, to thrust herself forward with her sin, she who should hide herself from the eyes of all people in a remote place of the world. She could have traveled all over the world and been certain of finding nowhere so severe a

5. See Luke 7:37–38.
6. See John 3:20.

judgment as the one that awaited her in the Pharisee's house from the proud Pharisees. On the other hand, there is perhaps no suffering so designed to torture precisely a woman as the cruelty of the mockery that awaited her in the Pharisee's house from the proud Pharisees. But she—is there no compassion that spares her this cruelty? no, there is no compassion!—she hated herself: she loved much.

She went in to the Holy One in the Pharisee's house, *to the feast.* To a feast! You shudder, you shrink from following her; you are easily convinced of how appalling it is, for you will be constantly tempted to forget that the whole thing takes place at a feast, that it is not a "house of mourning" but a "house of feasting."[7] At a feast a woman enters; she brings with her an alabaster jar of ointment—yes, that is appropriate at a feast; she sits at the feet of one of the guests—and weeps: that is not appropriate at a feast. Truly, she disturbs the feast, this woman! Yes, but it did not disturb her, this woman who was a sinner, she who, surely not without shuddering, not without shrinking back, nevertheless went forward to the feast—and to confession. She hated herself: she loved much. Oh, nothing else rests as heavy upon a person as sin's heavy secret; there is only one thing that is heavier: to have to go to confession. Oh, no other secret is as frightful as the secret of sin; there is only one thing that is even more frightful: confession. Therefore human compassion has sympathetically devised something that can alleviate and assist this difficult delivery. At the holy place, where everything is quiet, earnest solemnity, and in a more hidden enclosure within it, where everything is silent like the grave and lenient like the judgment of the dead—there the sinner is offered an opportunity to confess his sin. And human compassion devised the alleviation that the one receiving the confession was hidden, so that the sight of him would not make it too heavy—yes, too heavy for the sinner to relieve his conscience. Finally human compassion found that such a confession or such a hidden listener was not even needed; the confession should only be made in secret before God,[8] who after all knows everything anyway,[9] and could then remain hidden in one's innermost being. But at a feast—and a woman! A feast; it is not some hidden, out-of-the-way place, nor is the lighting semi-dark, nor is the mood like that among graves, and the hearers are neither silent nor invisibly

7. See Ecclesiastes 7:2.
8. See Matthew 6:6.
9. See 1 John 3:20.

present. No, if concealment and twilight and remoteness and every-thing connected with confessing one's sin is alleviation, a feast would surely be the cruelest device. Who then is this cruel person, that we by our prayers might mollify him so as to be lenient with her? No, no device of cruelty was so cruel; she alone, the woman who was a sinner, devised such a thing; she—oh, but ordinarily the cruel person is one, the tortured person another!—she herself devised the torture, was herself the cruel person; she hated herself: she loved much.

Yes, she loved much. "She sat at the feet of Christ, wet them with tears, dried them with her hair"—she is expressing: "I am capable of literally nothing at all, he is capable of absolutely everything." But this is indeed to love much. If one thinks oneself capable of something, I dare say one may love, but one does not love much; and to the degree that one thinks oneself capable of more, to the same degree one loves less. She, on the contrary, loved much. She makes not a sound; nei-ther does she make assurances—oh, simply far too often a deceitful expression so easily necessitates a new assurance that it actually is as one assures. She does not make assurances, she acts: she weeps, she kisses his feet. She does not think of checking her tears, no, weeping is after all her task. She weeps; it is not her eyes that she dries with her hair, it is his feet—she is capable of literally nothing at all, he absolutely everything—she loved much. Oh eternal truth, that he is capable of ab-solutely everything; oh indescribable truth in this woman; oh the inde-scribable power of truth in this woman, who powerfully expresses the powerlessness that she is capable of literally nothing: she loved much.

Yes, she loved much. She sits weeping at his feet—she has entirely forgotten herself, forgotten every disturbing thought in her own inner being, is entirely quiet, or quieted like a sick child is quieted at the mother's breast, where it cries itself out and forgets itself. For one does not succeed in forgetting such thoughts and still remember oneself; if one is to succeed, one must forget oneself—therefore she weeps, and as she weeps she forgets herself. Oh blessed tears, oh that in weeping there is also this blessing—there is oblivion! She has entirely forgotten herself, forgotten the setting with all its disturbing elements, for it is impossible to forget such a setting if one does not forget oneself; it was indeed a setting frightfully and agonizingly designed to remind her of herself—but she weeps, and already as she weeps she forgets herself. Oh blessed tears of self-forgetfulness when her weeping does not once remind her anymore of what she is weeping over; in this way she has entirely forgotten herself.

But the true expression for loving much, after all, is just to forget oneself entirely. If one remembers oneself, one may well love but does not love much; and the more one remembers oneself, to the same degree one loves less. Yet she has entirely forgotten herself. But the greater the impulse is at that very moment to remember or to think about oneself—if one nevertheless forgets oneself and thinks of the other, the more one loves. For instance, that is indeed the case in relation to love between human beings; even though these relations do not entirely correspond to what the discourse here is about, they can still shed light on it. The one who, at the moment when he is most preoccupied, at the moment most precious to himself, forgets himself and thinks of another, he loves much; the one who, being hungry himself, forgets himself and gives the other the meager supply that is only enough for one, he loves much; the one who in mortal danger forgets himself and lets the other have the only hope, he loves much. So also the one who, at the moment when everything in his own inner being and everything round about him not only reminds him of himself but wants to compel him against his will to remember himself—if he nevertheless forgets himself, he loves much, just as she did.

"She sits at his feet, anoints them with ointment, dries them with her hair, kisses them—and weeps." She says nothing and therefore is not what she says, but she is what she does not say, or what she does not say is what she is; she *is* the symbol, like a picture—she has forgotten speech and language and the restlessness of thought and, what is even more restlessness, has forgotten this self, forgotten herself, she the lost woman, who is now lost in her savior, lost in him resting at his feet—like a picture. And it is almost as if for a moment the savior himself looked at her and the situation in this way, as if she were not an actual person but a picture. No doubt in order to make the application to those present all the more penetrating, he does not speak *to* her; he does not say, "You are forgiven your many sins because you have loved much." He speaks *about* her; he says: "Her many sins are forgiven her because she loved much." Although she is present, it is almost as if she were absent, it is almost as if he transformed her into a picture, a parable, almost as if he said: "Simon, I have something to tell you.[10] There was once a woman; she was a sinner. When the Son of Man sat at dinner in the house of a Pharisee one day, she too came

10. See Luke 7:40.

in. The Pharisees mocked and judged her, saying that she was a sinner. But she sat by his feet, anointed them with ointment, dried them with her hair, kissed them and wept—Simon, I want to tell you something: her many sins were forgiven her because she loved much." It is almost like a story, a sacred story, a parable—and yet at the same moment the same thing was actually happening on the spot.

But *"her many sins were indeed also forgiven her"*—and how could this be expressed more strongly, more truly than by the fact that everything is forgotten, that she the great sinner is transformed into a picture. When "your sins are forgiven you" is said, oh how readily the recollection of herself then returns to her if she was not first strengthened by this infinite oblivion: her many sins were forgiven her. "She loved much," therefore she forgot herself entirely; she forgot herself entirely, "therefore her many sins were forgiven her"—forgotten, yes, they were drowned with her, so to speak, in an oblivion, she is transformed into a picture, she becomes a recollection, yet not so that it reminds her of herself, no, just as she forgot the recollection by forgetting herself, it has also, not eventually but immediately, forgotten what she is called; her name is: the woman who was a sinner, neither more nor less.

And were someone now to say, "there was nevertheless something self-loving in this woman's love; indeed, the Pharisees also took exception to her drawing near to Christ and inferred from this something disparaging about him, that he was no prophet[11]—thus she exposed him to this, she with her love, that is, with her self-love." Were someone to say, "there was nevertheless something self-loving in this woman's love; after all, in her need she still basically loved herself." Were someone to speak this way, then I would reply, "naturally," and then add, "worse luck; well, that's the way it is"—and then add, "God forbid that I might ever be tempted to want to love my God or my Savior differently, for if there was nothing in the sense of self-love in my love, then I would indeed be imagining that I could love them without needing them—and from this presumption may God preserve me!"

My listener, this woman was a sinner. The Pharisees judged her, they even judged Christ for being willing to have anything to do with her; they judged—and precisely for this reason—that he was no prophet, not to speak of savior of the world, whereas precisely by this

---

11. See Luke 7:39.

he manifested himself as the savior of the world. This woman was a sinner—yet she became and is a prototype; blessed is the one who resembles her in loving much! The forgiveness of sins which Christ offered while he lived continues from generation to generation to be offered to all in Christ. "Your sins are forgiven you" is said to all, each one individually. All, each one individually, receive at the altar the pledge that their sins are forgiven them—blessed is the one who resembles the woman who was a sinner in loving much! For even though it is said to all, it is still only true when it is said to the one who, like that woman, loved much! It is true, your sins are forgiven you in Christ; but this truth, which is therefore also said to each one individually, is in yet another sense still not true, it must be made true by each one individually. In this way that woman is an eternal picture; by her great love she made herself, if I dare say so, indispensable to the Savior. For that there is forgiveness of sins, which he purchased, she makes it true, she who loved much. You can therefore turn it however you will and still say basically the same thing. You can consider her blessed in that her many sins were forgiven her, and you can consider her blessed in that she loved much: basically you are saying the same thing—if you then note well that the one she loved much was precisely Christ, and if you then also do not forget that Christ is grace and the giver of grace.

Precisely what sort of a test is it in which her love is tried? With respect to what can she be said to love much? What is it she loves less? Is this the test: to love Christ more than father and mother,[12] gold and goods, honor and reputation? No, the test in which this woman is tried is: to love her Savior more than her sin. Oh, there was perhaps one who loved Christ more than father and mother and gold and goods and honor and life, and yet loved his sin more than his Savior, loved it, not in the sense of wanting to remain in it, to continue to sin, but in the sense of not really being willing to confess it. It is in a certain sense frightful but true, and everyone who has any knowledge of the human heart will verify it: there is nothing which a human being clings to so desperately as to his sin. And therefore a perfectly honest, deep, altogether true, entirely unsparing confession of sin is the perfect love; such a confession of sin is to love much.

Now the discourse is over. But is it not true, my listener, that even if the Pharisees have judged that this woman forced herself into a feast

12. See Matthew 10:37.

most improperly, today she has indeed not come to the wrong place, between the confessional and the altar! Oh, forget the orator who has spoken here, forget his artistry, that is, if he has shown any, forget his errors, which perhaps were many, forget the discourse about her—but do not forget her. On this path she is a guide, she who loved much and to whom therefore those many sins were forgiven. She is far from being some forbidding picture; on the contrary, she is more motivating than all the promptings of orators when it comes to following that invitation which leads to the altar: "Come here all you who labor and are heavy laden."[13] For she goes there at the head, she who loved much, she who therefore also found rest for her soul[14] in loving much, yes, or in her many sins being forgiven her, yes, or she who, because she loved much, found rest in this, that her many sins were forgiven her.

13. See Matthew 11:28.
14. See Matthew 11:29.

PART THREE

"From on High He Will Draw
All to Himself." First Christian
Exposition from *Practice
in Christianity*, No. III,
by Anti-Climacus (1850)

[11]

John 12:32[1]

Prayer

Lord Jesus Christ, there is so much to draw us back: empty exploits, trivial pleasures, unworthy concerns. There is so much to frighten us back: a pride that is too cowardly to let itself be helped, a cowardly timidity that shirks to its own destruction, an anxiety of sin [*en Syndens Angst*] that shuns the purity of holiness like sickness shuns the remedy. But you are indeed still the strongest: so draw us, and even more strongly, to yourself. We call you our Savior and Redeemer in that you came to the world in order to free us from the chains in which we were bound or in which we had bound ourselves, and in order to rescue the redeemed. This was your task, which you have completed and which you will complete until the end of time,[2] for just as you yourself have said it, so you will do it: lifted up from the earth, you will draw all to yourself.

John 12:32: And I, when I am lifted up from the earth, will draw all to myself.

From on high he will draw all to himself.
    Attentive listener, if a human being's life is not to be led altogether unworthily like that of the animal, which never lifts up its head; if it

---

1. [*Editor's note:*] The following note is appended to the text by Anti-Climacus, the pseudonymous author of *Practice in Christianity:* "This discourse was delivered by Magister Kierkegaard in Our Lady's Church on Friday, 1 September 1848. Since it originally gave me the idea for the title, I have printed it with his permission. In order to round off the whole with a conclusion that corresponds to this beginning, I have kept no. 7 in the same more lenient tone and to that extent have given up a portion of my character." No. 7 refers to the seventh discourse of No. III in *Practice in Christianity.*
    2. See John 17:4.

is not to be frittered away, emptily occupied with what is vanity as long as it lasts and is nothing when it is over, or busily occupied with what no doubt makes a noise at the moment but does not resonate in eternity—if a human being's life is not to be dozed away in idleness or wasted in bustle, then there must be something higher that draws it. Now this higher something can be quite varied; but if this higher something is to be truly and at every moment able to draw, it must not itself be subject to variation or change[3] but must triumphantly have gone through every change, transfigured—like the transfigured life of one who is dead. And just as there is now among all the living only one name that is named, the Lord Jesus Christ,[4] so there is also only one dead person who still lives, the Lord Jesus Christ, he who from *on high* will draw all to himself. See, a Christian's life, properly structured, is therefore directed toward what is above,[5] toward loftiness, toward him who from on high draws the Christian to himself—if the Christian remembers him, and the person who does not do that is certainly no Christian. And you, my listener, you to whom my discourse is addressed, you have indeed come here today precisely in *remembrance* of him.

It follows as a matter of course that if from on high he is able to draw the Christian to himself, there is much that must be forgotten, much that must be disregarded, much that must be died away from [*afdøes fra*].[6] How can this be done? Oh, if you have ever been concerned, perhaps concerned about your future, your success in life, have truly wished to be able to forget something—a disappointed expectation, a shattered hope, a bitter and embittering recollection; or if, alas, out of concern for the salvation of your soul, you have quite fervently wished to be able to forget something—an anxiety of sin that continually confronted you, a terrifying thought that would not leave you—then you yourself have no doubt experienced how empty is the advice the world gives when it says, "try to forget it!" For when you anxiously ask "how shall I go about forgetting?" and the reply is "you must try to forget," this is only an empty mockery, if it is anything at all. No, if there is something you want to forget, try to find something else to remember, then you will certainly succeed. If Christianity therefore requires of

---

3. See James 1:17.
4. See Philippians 2:9–11; Ephesians 1:20–21.
5. See Colossians 3:1–2.
6. Or "died to," as in Romans 6:2 and Colossians 2:20.

the Christian that he must forget much, and in a certain sense everything, namely the manifold, then it also recommends the means: to
remember something else, to bear in mind one thing, the Lord Jesus
Christ. If you then observe that the world's pleasures captivate you—
and you wish to forget; if you observe that worldly worry occupies
you so that you wish to forget; if you observe that the bustle of life
takes hold of you like the current carries the swimmer and you wish
to forget; if the anxieties of temptation pursue you and you fervently
wish to be able to forget—then remember him, the Lord Jesus Christ,
and you will no doubt succeed. Yes, just as today you now eat of the
bread and drink of the wine in remembrance of him, if in this way the
remembrance of him could remain in your thoughts every day so that
you remembered him in everything you did—then you would also
entirely have forgotten everything that should be forgotten; in relation
to everything that should be forgotten you would become as forgetful
as a feeble old man, as forgetful as one who in a foreign land has forgotten his mother tongue and speaks it meaninglessly, as forgetful as
an absent-minded person—you would be entirely drawn to the higher
by him who from on high will draw all to himself.

From on high he will draw all to himself.

From on high, for here on earth he walked in lowliness, in the
lowly form of a servant,[7] in poverty and wretchedness, a sufferer. This
indeed was Christianity, not that a rich man makes the poor rich but
that the poorest of all makes all rich, both the rich and the poor. And
this indeed was Christianity, not that it is the happy person who consoles the sorrowful but the one most sorrowful of all. He will draw all
to himself; *draw* them to himself, for he will *entice* no one to himself.
Truly to draw to oneself is in one sense to thrust aside. There is much
in your being as in mine and that of every human being that he wants
to have removed; as regards all that, he will thrust aside. Lowliness,
abasement is the stumbling block,[8] the possibility of offense, and you
are situated between his abasement, which lies behind, and his loftiness—precisely for that reason he is said to draw to himself. To entice
to oneself is untruthfully to draw to oneself, but he will entice no
one, abasement belongs to him just as essentially as loftiness. If there
were one who could only love him in his loftiness, such a person's

---

7. See Philippians 2:7.
8. See 1 Corinthians 1:23; Romans 9:32–33; 1 Peter 2:7–8.

view is confused; he does not know Christ, therefore neither does he love him, he takes him in vain. Christ was and is indeed the truth.[9] If then someone can only love him in his loftiness, what does that mean? It means he can only love the truth—when it has conquered, when it is in possession of and surrounded by power and honor and glory.[10] But when it struggled, when it was foolishness, an offense to the Jews, a folly to the Greeks,[11] when it was insulted, mocked, and as the scripture says, spat upon,[12] then such a person consequently could not love it, then he wished to stay far away. That is, he wished the truth far away from him, but this is indeed precisely to be in untruth. It is just as essential for "the truth" to suffer in this world as to triumph in another world, the world of truth—and Christ Jesus is the same in his abasement as in his loftiness. But if, on the other hand, someone could only feel drawn to Christ and love him in his abasement, if such a person wanted to hear nothing at all about his loftiness, when power and honor and glory are his; if he (oh pitiful perversity!) with the impatience of a restless spirit, bored, as he no doubt would say, by Christendom's good and victorious days, if he merely longed for the scene of horror, to be with him when he was being derided and persecuted—then the vision of such a person is also confused, he does not know Christ; consequently neither does he love him. For melancholy is no closer to Christianity than frivolity; they are both equally worldliness, equally far away, equally as much in need of conversion.[13]

My listener, you to whom my discourse is addressed, you who today have come here in remembrance of him, our Lord Jesus Christ, you have thus come here drawn by him who from on high will draw all to himself. But precisely today you are reminded of his abasement, his suffering and death: so it is he who draws you to himself. He has not in loftiness forgotten you—and you do not forget his abasement; you love him in his abasement but in his glorious revelation as well.

From on high he will draw all to himself.

9. See John 14:6.
10. An allusion to the conclusion of the Lord's Prayer in Matthew 6:13 added by some ancient biblical authorities and included in the Danish Bible of 1819 and church ritual books used by Kierkegaard. See SKS K 12:204, note to line 2.
11. See 1 Corinthians 1:23.
12. See Luke 18:32; 22:63, 65; 23:11, 39; Matthew 27:29–30, 39, 41; Mark 15:19–20, 32.
13. See Luke 15:7.

It is now eighteen centuries since he left the earth and ascended on high.[14] Since that time the shape of the world has changed more than once; thrones have risen and fallen, great names have emerged and been forgotten; and in smaller matters, in our daily life, the usual things occur, the sun comes up and goes down, the wind changes by turns, something new is heard and soon forgotten again, and then something new again[15]—but from him, in a certain sense, nothing is heard. And yet he has said that from on high he will draw all to himself. So he is not resting on high,[16] but he is working,[17] occupied with and concerned about drawing all to himself. Wonderful! Yet you likewise see many forces in nature stirring around you; but the power that supports everything you do not see, you do not see God's omnipotence—and yet it is indeed just as fully certain that he too is working, that one single instant without him the world is then nothing. He is likewise invisible on high, yet everywhere present, occupied with drawing all to himself—alas, while in the world there is mundane talk of everything else, as if he did not exist at all. He uses the most diverse things as a way and means of drawing to himself; but we cannot develop this here, least of all today, when only an unusually brief period is prescribed for the discourse because the sacred act is the chief concern and Holy Communion is the divine service. But even though the means he uses are ever so many, all the ways still converge at one point: the consciousness of sin; through it is "the way"[18] by which he draws a person, the penitent, to himself.

My listener, you to whom my discourse is addressed, you who have come here today in remembrance of him in order to participate in the sacred meal of the Lord's Supper, you went first, of course, to confession today—before you now go up to the altar. From on high he has drawn you to himself, but through the consciousness of sin. He leads the single individual to this place by many, very different ways, but he draws him to himself only by one way: through the consciousness of sin. For he will entice no one to himself but will draw all to himself.

From on high he will draw all to himself.

14. See Luke 24:50–51; Acts 1:9–11.
15. See Ecclesiastes 1:4–10.
16. See Hebrews 4:1–11; Genesis 2:2–3.
17. See John 5:17.
18. See John 14:6.

My listener, you, to whom my discourse is addressed! Today he is indeed with you as if he were closer to the earth, as if he were, so to speak, touching the earth; he is present at the altar where you seek him; he is present there—but only in order once again from on high to draw you to himself. For because you feel yourself drawn to him and therefore have come here today, from that it still does not follow that you dare think that he has already drawn you *entirely* to himself. "Lord, increase my faith."[19] The person who prayed this prayer was not an unbeliever but a believer; so also with this prayer: "Lord, draw me entirely to yourself."[20] The one who shall rightly pray this prayer must already feel himself drawn. Oh, and is it not true, just today and just because you feel yourself drawn today, just for that reason you would no doubt be willing today to confess to yourself and to him how much is still left, how far it is from being the case that he has entirely drawn you to himself—from on high, away from everything base and worldly that would hold you back. Oh, my listener, it certainly is not me nor any other human being who says or will say or dares say this to you; no, every human being will have enough with saying it to himself— and should have praise for God if he is ever sufficiently moved to say it to himself. My listener, I do not know where you are, how far he has perhaps already drawn you to himself, how far more advanced in being a Christian you perhaps are than I and so many others, but God grant that this day, wherever you are and whoever you are, you who have come here today in order to participate in the sacred meal of the Lord's Supper, that this day may truly be blessed for you. God grant that at this sacred moment you may feel yourself entirely drawn to him, sense his presence, he who is present there, he from whom you are then indeed separated when you leave the altar, but who surely will not forget you if you do not forget him, yes, will not forget you even if, alas, you sometimes were to forget him, who from on high continues to draw you to himself until the last blessed end when you one day shall be with him and with him on high.

19. See Luke 17:5.
20. A line from a psalm by Hans Adolph Brorson in *Psalmer og aandelige Sange,* 2 vols. (Kiøbenhavn: J. A. L. Holm, 1838), no. 104, p. 322 (ASKB Appendix 1, no. 90).

PART FOUR

Two Discourses at the Communion on Fridays
(1851)

TO ONE UNNAMED,
whose name one day will be named,

is dedicated
with this little work the whole authorship,
as it was from the beginning.[1]

Preface

A gradually advancing author-activity that began with *Either/Or* seeks here its decisive point of rest at the foot of the altar, where the author, personally most conscious of his own imperfection and guilt, by no means calls himself a truth-witness but only a singular kind of poet and thinker who, "without authority," has had nothing new to bring but "has wanted to read through once again, if possible in a more inward way, the original text of the individual human existence-relationships, the old, familiar text handed down from the fathers" (see my postscript to *Concluding Unscientific Postscript*).[2]

---

1. A dedication to Kierkegaard's former fiancée, Regine Schlegel, née Olsen (1822–1904).
2. See CUP 1:629–30.

In this direction, I have nothing further to add. However, let me merely say this, which in a way is my life, to me the content of my life, its fullness, its happiness, its peace and satisfaction—this or this life-view, which is the thought of humanity and human equality: Christianly, every human being (the single individual), absolutely every human being, once again, absolutely every human being is equally near to God; and how near and equally near? In being loved by him. Thus there is equality, the infinite equality between human beings. If there is any difference, oh, this difference, if it exists, is like peacefulness itself; undisturbed, it does not in the remotest way disturb the equality. The difference is: that one person bears in mind that he is loved, perhaps day in and day out, perhaps for 70 years day in and day out, perhaps with only one longing, for eternity, in order properly to be able to get moving and rush on, busy with this blessed occupation of keeping in mind that he—alas, and not for the sake of his virtue!—is loved. Another person perhaps does not bear in mind that he is loved, perhaps goes year after year, day after day, and does not bear in mind that he is loved, or he is perhaps glad and thankful for being loved by his wife, by his children, by friends, by contemporaries, but he does not bear in mind that he is loved by God, or he perhaps sighs over not being loved by anyone, and he does not bear in mind that he is loved by God. "Yet," so might the first person very well say, "I am innocent; after all, I am not to blame if another person disregards or disdains the love that is lavished just as richly upon him as upon me." Infinite, divine love, which makes no distinction![3] Alas—human ingratitude!— what if there were then an equality between us human beings in which we entirely resemble one another, so that none of us properly bears in mind that he is loved!

As I turn then in another direction, I would wish and would permit myself (giving thanks for the sympathy and good will that may have been shown to me), as it were, to present and to commend these works to the people whose language I with filial devotion and with almost feminine infatuation am proud of having the honor to write, yet also consoling myself that it will not have been dishonored by the fact that I have written it.

Copenhagen, late summer 1851   S. K.

3. See Deuteronomy 10:17; 2 Chronicles 19:7; Job 34:19; Acts 10:34; Romans 2:11; Galatians 2:6; 1 Peter 1:17.

[12]

Luke 7:47

Prayer

Lord Jesus Christ! You who certainly did not come to the world in order to judge,[1] yet by being love that was not loved, you were a judgment upon the world. We call ourselves Christians, we say that we know no one to go to except you—alas, to whom should we then go[2] when precisely by your love the judgment also comes upon us that we love little? To whom, oh hopelessness, if after all not to you; to whom, oh despair, if you really would not receive us mercifully, forgiving our great sin against you and against love, we who sinned much by loving little!

Luke 7:47: But [the one] to whom little is forgiven loves little.[3]

Attentive listener, at the altar the invitation, "come here all you who labor and are heavy laden, I will give you rest,"[4] is indeed given. The single individual then accepts the invitation; he goes up to the altar. After that he comes back, leaving the altar—then there is another text, it could be inscribed over the church door inside, not to be read by those who are entering the church but only by those who are leaving the church, this text: "[the one] to whom little is forgiven loves little." The first text is the altar's invitation; the other is the altar's justifica-

---

1. See John 3:17–19, 12:47.
2. See John 6:68.
3. Cited from the 1819 Danish edition of the New Testament, with the capitalization of "but" added and the comma after "forgiven" left out. See SKS K12:365, line 11.
4. See Matthew 11:28.

tion, as if it were said there: "If at the altar you were not sensible of the forgiveness of your sins, every one of your sins, then it is due to yourself; the communion is without blame, the blame is yours, because you only loved little." Oh, just as it is a difficult matter in praying rightly to be able to come to the Amen—for the one who has never prayed it seems easy enough, easy enough to be finished quickly; but for the one who felt a need to pray and began to pray, it surely has happened that it continually seemed to him as if he had something more upon his heart, as if he could neither get everything said nor get it all said as he wished it said, and thus he does not get to the Amen—likewise it is also a difficult matter rightly to receive the forgiveness of sins at the altar. There the gracious forgiveness of all your sins is pledged to you. If you hear it rightly, take the forgiveness of all your sins quite literally, then you will be able to go away from the altar, divinely understood, as light of heart as a newborn child, upon whom nothing, nothing weighs heavily, thus even lighter of heart insofar as much has weighed upon your heart. At the altar there is no one who would spare you even the least of your sins, no one—if you yourself do not do it. So cast them all away from you; and the recollection of them—lest you retain them in that; and the recollection of having thrown them away—lest you retain them within yourself in that. Cast it all away from you; you have nothing at all to do except, believing, to cast away from yourself and to cast away from yourself what weighs heavily and burdens. What could be easier! Ordinarily the difficult thing is to have to take burdens upon oneself, but to dare, to have to cast away from oneself! And yet how difficult! Yes, even rarer than the one who shouldered all burdens, even rarer is the one who accomplished the apparently very easy task, after having received the assurance of the gracious forgiveness of his sins and the pledge of it, of feeling entirely relieved of every—even the least sin, or of every—even the greatest sin! If you could peer into hearts you would no doubt see how many go up to the altar burdened, groaning under the heavy burden; and when they then leave there, if you could peer into hearts you would possibly see that basically there was not a single one who went away entirely relieved, and sometimes you would perhaps see that there was one who went away even more burdened, burdened by the thought that he surely had not been a worthy guest at the altar since he found no relief.

That this is so we shall not conceal from one another; we shall not speak in such a way that the discourse appears ignorant of how things happen in actuality, depicts everything so perfectly that it does not apply at all to us actual human beings. Oh no, how then would the discourse be of help? On the contrary, however, if the discourse makes us as imperfect as we are, then it helps us to be kept in a constant striving, neither intoxicated in dreams that make us believe that everything was decided by this one time nor give up in quiet despondency because this time it did not come off according to our wish, did not happen as we had prayed and desired.

Let us then in the prescribed brief moments consider this text: "But [the one] to whom little is forgiven loves little," a *word of judgment* but also a *word of consolation.*

And you, my listener, do not be disturbed at my speaking in this way at this moment before you go up to the altar, perhaps thinking and insisting that the one who is to speak at this moment should speak in a different manner, employing everything to reassure the single individual and make him confident; if he then learned later that the holy act still had not been entirely a joy and blessing to an individual, he could then of course speak to him in a different manner. O my friend, in part it truly is not so that it is only a single individual who does not succeed to perfection, no, it is only a single individual who does succeed to perfection; in part there is a concern, a heartfelt concern that perhaps helps a person to succeed better in the highest sense, better than too much confidence and too carefree frankness. There is a longing for God, a confidence in God, a trust, a hope in God, a love, a frankness: but what most surely finds him is perhaps a sorrowing for God;[5] a sorrowing for God—that is no transient mood which immediately disappears as one draws nearer to God; on the contrary, it is perhaps deepest just when one draws nearest to God, just as the sorrowing person is likewise most fearful for himself the nearer he comes to God.

[*The one*] *to whom little is forgiven loves little.* This is the word of judgment.

Generally it is no doubt described this way: justice is the severe judgment; love is the leniency that does not judge, and if it does judge, love's judgment is the lenient judgment. No, no, love's judgment is the severest judgment. Was not the severest judgment that was passed upon the world, more severe than the flood,[6] more severe than Babel's

---

5. See 2 Corinthians 7:9–10.
6. See Genesis 6:1–9:29.

confusion of tongues,[7] more severe than the destruction of Sodom and Gomorrah,[8] was it not Christ's innocent death,[9] which yet was love's sacrifice? And what was the judgment? Well surely this: "Love" was not loved. So also here. The word of judgment does not say: "[The one] to whom little is forgiven sinned much, so his sins were therefore too great and too many to be forgiven." No, judgment says: "He loves little." Thus it is not justice that severely denies the forgiveness and pardoning of sins; it is love that leniently and mercifully says: "*I* forgive you everything—if you are forgiven only little, then it is because you only love little." Justice sets strict boundaries and says: "No further, that is the limit;[10] for you there is no forgiveness," but with that it also stands. Love says: "Everything is forgiven you—if you are only forgiven little, then it is because you only love little." So then there comes a new sin, a new guilt, that of becoming guilty of only being forgiven little, becoming guilty not by those past sins but by the lack of love. If you want to learn to fear, then learn to fear not the severity of justice but the leniency of love!

Justice looks judgingly upon a person, and the sinner cannot endure its glance; but when love looks at him, yes, even if he avoids its glance, casts his eyes down,[11] he nevertheless still perceives that it is looking at him, for love presses far more intimately into life, in close to life, in there whence life originates, than does justice, which repellently confirms the yawning abyss[12] between the sinner and itself, whereas love is indeed on his side, does not accuse, does not judge, pardons and forgives. The sinner cannot endure the judging voice of justice; he seeks, if possible, to shut his ears to it; but even if he wanted to, it is impossible for him not to hear the love whose judgment, oh frightful judgment, is: "Your sins are forgiven you!" Frightful judgment, whose word in itself is surely anything but terrifying; and precisely for that reason the sinner cannot refrain from hearing what nevertheless is judgment there. Where shall I flee from justice? If I take the wings of the morning and fly to the farthest sea,[13] it is there, and if I hide in the abyss, it is there, and likewise in every place; yet no, there is

---

7. See Genesis 11:1–9.
8. See Genesis 18:16–19:28.
9. See Luke 23:4, 41; Matthew 27:4, 19, 23–24.
10. See. Job 38:8–11.
11. See Luke 18:13.
12. See Luke 16:26.
13. See Psalms 139:7–10.

one place to which I can flee: to love. But when love judges you, and the judgment is—oh horror!—the judgment is: "Your sins are forgiven you!" Your sins are forgiven you—and yet there is something (yes, this something is within you, where else in the world would it find its abode when love forgives everything!), there is something within you that makes you feel that they are not forgiven you. What then is the horror of the severest judgment in comparison to this horror! What then is the severe judgment of wrath, the curse, in comparison to this judgment: "Your sins are forgiven you!" So justice is indeed almost leniency that says, as you say: "No, they are not forgiven you!" What is the suffering of "the fratricide"[14] when he, inconstant and unsteady, fears that everyone will recognize him by the mark of justice that condemned him—what is this suffering in comparison to the anguish of the unhappy person for whom these words became judgment, not salvation: "Your sins are forgiven you!" What frightful severity! That love, that it is love, the forgiving love which, not censoriously, no, alas, itself suffering in so doing, is nevertheless changed into judgment; that love, the forgiving love, which does not want like justice to make the guilt manifest but on the contrary wants to hide it[15] by forgiving and pardoning, is nevertheless the one which, alas, itself suffering in so doing, makes the guilt more frightfully manifest than does justice!

Ponder this thought: "the self-inflicted." "It is self-inflicted," says justice, "that there is no forgiveness for a person"; thereby it thinks of his many sins, for justice can forget nothing. Love says: "It is self-inflicted"—thereby it thinks not of his many sins, oh no, it is willing to forget them all, it has forgotten them all; and yet, "it is self-inflicted," says love. Which is the more frightful? Surely the latter, which indeed almost sounds like demented talk, for the charge is not his sins, no, the charge is: it is forgiven him, everything is forgiven him. Think of a sinner who is sinking in the abyss; listen to his anguished cry when with his last sigh he lets justice, which his life has mocked, give him his due and say: "It is self-inflicted." Frightful! There is only one thing more frightful, if it is not to justice he speaks but to love and says: "It is self-inflicted." Justice is not mocked,[16] verily, love even less. More severe than justice's severest judgment of the greatest sinner is that of love: he is forgiven little—because he only loved little.

14. See Genesis 4:1–16.
15. See 1 Peter 4:8.
16. See Galatians 6:7.

[*The one*] *to whom little is forgiven loves little.* This is a word of judgment, but also a word of *consolation.*

I do not know, my listener, what your crime, your guilt, your sins are, but surely the guilt we are all more or less guilty of is only to love little. So be consoled then by the text, just as I am consoled by it. And how am I consoled? I am consoled by the fact that the text after all says nothing about divine love but only something about mine. The text does not say that the divine love has now become weary of being love, that it has now changed, weary of squandering, as it were, indescribable mercy upon the ungrateful race of human beings or upon me the ungrateful one, that it has now become something else, a lesser love, its fervor cooled because the love became cold in the ungrateful race of human beings or in me the ungrateful one. No, the text does not speak about that at all. So be consoled, just as I am consoled—by what? By this, that the reason the text does not say it is that the holy text does not lie, so it has not then accidently or cruelly been suppressed in the text while in actuality it is really so that God's love has become weary of loving. No, if the text does not say it, then neither is it so; and even if the text said it—no the text could not say it, for the text cannot lie. Oh, in the deepest sorrow the most blessed consolation! If God's love had in truth changed, if you had heard nothing about it but were concerned about yourself, that until now you had only loved little, with devout resolve had striven to bring the love within you to blaze and you fed the flame in the same way you brought it to blaze— and now, even though you felt ashamed of how imperfect your love still was, you wanted to draw near to God in order, according to the words of scripture, to be reconciled with him[17]—but he had changed!

Imagine a girl in love; concerned, she confesses to herself how little she has really loved until now—"so now then," she says to herself, "I will in turn become sheer love." And she succeeds. These tears of concern she shed in sorrow over herself, these tears—they do not put out the fire, no, they are too hot for that; oh no, precisely these tears make the fire blaze—but meanwhile the beloved had changed, he was no longer loving. Oh, one concern for a human being! Oh, for a human being one concern can be enough, more no human being can bear. Should a human being, inasmuch as he must in self-concern confess to himself how little he has loved God until now, be troubled by the

---

17. See 2 Corinthians 5:20.

thought whether God meanwhile could have changed—then, yes then
I will despair, and I will despair at once, for then there is nothing more
to wait for, neither in time nor in eternity. But for that reason I am
consoled by the text; and I block every evasion for myself, and I clear
away all excuses and extenuations and bare my breast, where I shall be
wounded by the text that censoriously forces its way in, judging[18] "you
loved only little." Oh, only penetrate more deeply, even more deeply,
you healing pain: "You did not love at all." Even when the judgment
goes this way, in a certain sense I feel no pain, I feel an indescribable
blessedness, for precisely my sentence, the sentence of death upon me
and my paltry love, implies something else: God is unchanged love.[19]

In this way I am consoled. And I find hidden in the text a consolation which you, my listener, no doubt also find precisely when you
hear the text in such a way that it wounds you. For it does not say, "[the
one] to whom little is forgiven *loved* little," no, it says: *loves* little. Oh,
when justice judges, it balances the account, closes it; it uses the past
tense, saying "he *loved* little," and means thereby that now the matter
is forever settled, we two are separated, have nothing more to do with
each other. The text, the word of love, however, goes: "[The one] to
whom little is forgiven, he loves little." He loves little; he *loves;* that is
to say: this is the way it is now, now at this instant—love does not say
more; infinite love, that in this way you remain true to yourself even in
your slightest utterance! He loves little now, at this instant. But what is
the now, and what is the instant?—swiftly, swiftly it is past; and now, at
the next instant, now everything is changed, now he loves, even if not
much, yet he is striving to love much; now everything is changed, but
not "love," it is unchanged, the same unchanged love that lovingly has
waited on him, lovingly has not had the heart to be finished with him,
has not had the heart to seek a separation from him but has remained
with him. And now it is not justice that conclusively says "he loved
little"; now it is love that joyfully in heaven[20] says "he loved little, that
is, now it is different, times have changed, now, now he loves much."

But is it then really not so after all that the forgiveness of sin *is
merited,* admittedly not by works but by love? When it is said that the
one to whom little is forgiven loves little, is it not implied that it is love

18. See Hebrews 4:12.
19. See 1 John 4:8, 16.
20. See Luke 15:7.

that makes the decision whether and how one's sins should be forgiv-
en—and thus the forgiveness of sins is indeed *merited*? Oh no. In the
same gospel a little earlier (v. 42 to the end) Christ speaks about two
debtors, one of whom owed much, the other little, and both of whom
found forgiveness. He asks: "Which of these two ought to love the
most?" And the answer is: "The one to whom much was forgiven."[21]
Now pay attention to how we still do not enter the hapless region of
merit but how everything remains within love! When you love much,
you are forgiven much—and when you are forgiven much, you love
much. See here the blessed recurrence of salvation in love! First you
love much, and much is then forgiven you—oh, and see, love then gets
even stronger; this, that so much has been forgiven you, it loves forth
love once again, and you love much because much has been forgiven
you! Here love is like faith. Imagine one of those unfortunate persons
whom Christ healed by a miracle. In order to be healed, he must believe—now he believes and is healed.[22] Now he is healed—and now
faith becomes twice as strong now that he is saved. It is not like this:
he believed and then the miracle happened and then it was over. No,
the fulfillment doubles his faith; after the fulfillment his faith is twice
as strong as when he believed before he was saved. And it is like that
with this matter of loving much. The love that loves much and then is
forgiven much is strong, divinely strong in weakness,[23] but even stronger is love's second time, when the same love loves another time, loves
because much has been forgiven.

My listener, no doubt you remember the beginning of this discourse. At this solemn moment one can disturb in two ways: by speaking about something irrelevant, even though, as it happens, it is both
important and the discourse meaningful; or by speaking disturbingly
about that which at such a moment is closest to one. "[The one] to
whom little is forgiven loves little"—this could seem disturbing just at
this moment before you go up to the altar, where you indeed receive
the forgiveness of all your sins. Oh, but just as the upbuilding is always
terrifying at first, and just as all true love is always unrest at first, and
just as love of God is always sorrow at first, so what seems disturbing
is not always disturbing; what is truly quieting is always disquieting

21. See Luke 7:41–43.
22. See Matthew 9:27–31; John 9:1–41.
23. See 2 Corinthians 12:9–10.

at first. But is there any comparison between these two dangers—that of being quieted in fraudulent security and that of being disquieted by being reminded of the disquieting thought? Now of what disquieting thought? Of *the* disquieting thought: that if one until now has only loved little, this too can be forgiven. The disquieting is peculiar; it is true that the one who is properly educated by it does not seem as strong as the one who remained ignorant of it. But at the last instant when he, precisely by his impotence, is after all perhaps the strongest, at the last instant, precisely by his impotence he perhaps succeeds where the strongest fails.

So, then, may God bless this disquieting discourse, that it may have disquieted you only for the good, that you, quieted by the Holy Communion, may feel that you receive gracious forgiveness of all your sins.

[13]

1 Peter 4:8

Prayer

Lord Jesus Christ! The birds had nests, the foxes had holes, and you had nowhere you could lay your head;[1] you were homeless in the world—yet were yourself the hiding place, the only one where the sinner could flee. Oh, and likewise this very day you are the hiding place; when the sinner flees to you, hides himself in you, is hidden in you[2]— then he is kept eternally safe, then "Love" hides a multitude of sins.

1 Peter 4:8:[3] Love will hide a multitude of sins.[4]

This applies in a double sense when the discourse is about human love, as we have explained further elsewhere.[5] The one in whom there is love, the loving person, hides a multitude of sins, does not see the neighbor's faults, or if he sees them, he is still as one who does not see them, hides them from himself and from others; love, in an even more beautiful sense than infatuation, makes him blind, blind to the neighbor's sins.[6] On the other hand, the one in whom there is love, the loving person, even if, as it happens, he also has faults, imperfections, yes, even if his sins were manifold—love, the fact that there is love in him, covers a multitude of sins.

When the discourse is about Christ's love, then the text can be taken in only one sense; that he was love did not serve to hide what

1. See Matthew 8:20; Luke 9:58.
2. See Colossians 3:3.
3. The Danish text erroneously says v. 7.
4. See also James 5:20.
5. See EUD, 55–78; WL, 280–99.
6. See EUD, 59; WL, 68.

imperfection there was in him—the holy one, in whom there was no sin and in whose mouth there was no deceit,[7] naturally, since in him there was only love, love in his heart and only love in his every word, in all his deeds, in his whole life, in his death, to the last. Oh, in a human being love is not so perfect; therefore he has or nevertheless derives, as it were, profit from it: while he lovingly hides a multitude of sins, love does in turn to him what he does to others, covers his sins. Thus he himself needs the love which he shows; thus he himself derives advantage from the love in him, which nevertheless, insofar as it turns outward, hiding a multitude of sins, does not, like Christ's sacrificial love, include the whole world, but only very few. Alas, even though it is rare enough that a human being is a loving person, what wonder, one could be tempted to say, what wonder that a human being strives to be that, he who himself needs love, and to that extent, by being loving, is still in a certain sense looking after his own interest. But Christ did not need love. Imagine that he had not been love; imagine that he in an unloving way only wanted to have been what he was, the Holy One; imagine that he, instead of saving the world and hiding a multitude of sins, had come to the world in holy wrath in order to judge the world.[8] In order to consider all the more fervently that even if it is true of him in just a single sense that his love hides a multitude of sins, imagine this, that *it* was "Love," that, as the scripture says, there is only one who is good:[9] God, that likewise he was, alone, the Loving One who hides a multitude of sins, not of some few individuals but of the whole world.

Let us then in the prescribed brief moments speak about this text:

Love (Christ's love) hides a multitude of sins.

And is it not true that you have felt the need for that, and precisely today, for a love that can cover sins, cover your sins—therefore you are indeed going up today to the Lord's altar. For while it is only too true what Luther says,[10] that every human being has a preacher within

7. See Hebrews 4:15; 1 Peter 2:22; Isaiah 53:9.
8. See John 3:17.
9. See Matthew 19:17.
10. See *The Complete Sermons of Martin Luther,* vol. 6, ed. Eugene F. A. Klug, trans. Eugene F. A. Klug, Erwin W. Koehlinger, James Lanning, Everette W. Meier, Dorothy Schoknecht, and Allen Schuldheiss (Grand Rapids, Mich.: Baker Books, 2000), 47; *En christelige Postille, sammendragen af Dr. Martin Luthers Kirke-og-Huus postiller,* trans. Jørgen Thisted, 2 vols. (København, 1828), 245 (ASKB, 283).

him who eats with him, drinks with him, wakes with him, sleeps with him, in short, is always about him, always with him, wherever he is, whatever he does, a preacher who is called flesh and blood, lusts and passions, habits and inclinations—so it is also certain that in the inmost recesses of every human being's heart there is a confidant that is just as scrupulously present everywhere: the conscience. A person can perhaps succeed in hiding his sins from the world; he can perhaps foolishly rejoice in his success, or yet, a little more truthfully, admit that it is a sorry weakness and cowardice that he does not have courage to become open—but a person cannot hide his sins from himself. That is impossible, for the sin that was altogether unconditionally hidden from the person himself would indeed not be sin, no more than if it were hidden from God, which is not the case either, since as soon as he is conscious of himself and in everything in which he is conscious of himself, a person is also conscious of God and God is conscious of him. And therefore he is so powerful and so scrupulous and always so present and so incorruptible because he is allied with God, this privy preacher who follows a person everywhere, when he wakes and when he sleeps (alas, if he does not make him sleepless by his preaching!), everywhere, in the din of the world (alas, if with his voice he does not transform the world's noise into stillness for him!), in solitude (alas, if he does not prevent him from feeling alone even in that most solitary place!), at the daily work (alas, if he does not make him therefore alienated and distracted!), in festive surroundings (alas, if he does not make them like a gloomy prison for him!), in holy places (alas, if he does not keep him from going there)—this privy preacher who accompanies the person, privy to what he now, now at this instant is doing or leaves undone, and to the longest, longest—no, not the longest forgotten, this confidant, which has a frightful memory, takes care of that—but the longest, longest time ago. A person can no more flee from this confidant than he can, according to that pagan's saying,[11] outride the care that sits behind on the horse, and no more than, if you want a different figure, no more than it "helps the deer to dash forward in order to run away from the arrow lodged in its breast—indeed, the more impetuously it behaves, the more firmly it merely runs the arrow into itself."[12]

11. See *Horace: The Odes and Epodes,* trans. C. E. Bennett (Cambridge, Mass.: Harvard University Press, 1978), 171.
12. A free rendition of a passage from *Fenelon's Werke religiösen Inhalts,* trans. Matthias Claudius, 3 vols. (Hamburg, 1822), I:219 (ASKB, 1914).

But today you are certainly also far from wanting to make the futile attempt to flee or to avoid this privy preacher; on the contrary, you have given him the floor. For in the confessional it is certainly the priest who preaches, but the true preacher is still the confidant in your inner being. The priest can only preach in a general way; the preacher in your inner being is just the opposite, he speaks simply and solely about you, to you, within you.

Being sufficiently dismayed myself, I will not make any attempt to dismay; but whoever you are, even if you are, humanly speaking, almost pure and innocent—when this privy preacher preaches to you in your inner being, then you too feel what others perhaps feel more dismayingly, you feel a need to hide yourself; and even if you were told thousands of times and thousands of times again that it is impossible to find this hiding place, you still feel the need. Oh, that I knew how to flee to a deserted island where no human being ever came or comes; oh, that there were a place of refuge where I likewise could flee, far away from myself; that there were a hiding place where I am so hidden that not even the consciousness of my sin can find me; that there were a boundary, even if ever so narrow, if it still makes a separation between my sin and me; that on the other side of a yawning abyss there were a spot, even if ever so small, where I could stand while the consciousness of my sin must remain on yonder side; that there were a forgiveness, a forgiveness that does not make my sense of guilt be increased but truly takes the guilt from me, also the consciousness of it; that there were an oblivion!

But now it is indeed so; for love (Christ's love) hides a multitude of sins. See, everything has become new![13] What in paganism was sought and sought in vain, what under the dominion of the law was and is a fruitless endeavor—the gospel made possible.[14] At the altar the Savior spreads his arms[15] and precisely for this fugitive who wants to flee from the consciousness of his sin, flee from what is even worse than being pursued, flee from what rankles. He opens his arms and says "come here to me"; and that he opens his arms already says "come here"; and that he, opening his arms, says "come here" also says: "Love hides a multitude of sins."

13. See 2 Corinthians 5:17.
14. See Romans 7; Galatians 3:23–24.
15. Probably another reference to the statue of Christ by the Danish sculptor Bertel Thorvaldsen that stands behind the altar of Our Lady's Church in Copenhagen with the words "COME UNTO ME" from Matthew 11:28 inscribed below.

Oh, believe him! Could you think the one who opens his redeeming arms to you, could you think him guilty of wordplay, think him capable of using a meaningless phrase, think him capable of deceiving you, and just at that moment—that he could say "come here," and at the moment you then came here and he held you in his embrace, that it would then be as if you were taken prisoner; for here, precisely here there would be no oblivion, here with—the Holy One! No, this you could not believe; and if you did believe it, you would certainly not come here—but blessed is the one[16] who quite literally believes that love (Christ's love) hides a multitude of sins. For a loving person, yes, even if it were the most loving, can lovingly judge with leniency, lovingly shut his eyes to your sins—oh, but he cannot shut your eyes to them. By loving speech and sympathy he can try to mitigate your guilt also in your own eyes and to that extent, as it were, hide it from you, or at least to a certain degree more or less hide it from you—oh, but actually to hide it from you, literally to hide it from you, so that it is hidden like what is hidden at the bottom of the sea and what no one ever gets to see any more, hidden so that what was red like blood becomes whiter than snow,[17] hidden so that sin is transformed into purity and you yourself dare to believe yourself justified and pure—that only he can do, the Lord Jesus Christ, whose love hides a multitude of sins. A human being has no authority, cannot command you to believe, and just by commanding with authority help you to believe. But if authority is required even to teach,[18] what authority, if possible greater than the one that commands the rough sea to be calm,[19] what authority is required for commanding the despairing person, the one who in the agony of repentance cannot and dare not forget, the contrite person who cannot and dare not stop staring at his guilt, what authority is required for commanding him to shut his eyes, and what authority for then commanding him to open the eyes of faith so that he may see purity where he saw guilt and sin! This divine authority he alone has, Jesus Christ, whose love hides a multitude of sins.

He hides it quite literally. Just as when one human being places himself in front of another human being and covers him completely with his body so that no one, no one can see the one who is hidden be-

---

16. See Matthew 5:3–11, 11:6.
17. See Isaiah 1:18; Psalm 51:7.
18. See Matthew 7:28–29.
19. See Matthew 8:23–27.

hind, so Jesus Christ covers your sin with his *holy body*. If justice were then to fly into a rage, what more does it want—there is indeed satisfaction. If the repentance within you then feels ever so heartrendingly that it should help the justice outside you to discover the guilt—there is indeed satisfaction, a satisfaction, one who makes satisfaction, who completely covers all your guilt and makes it impossible to see, impossible for justice and thereby in turn for the repentance within you or for you, for repentance also loses its sight when the justice to which it appeals says: "I can see nothing."

He hides it quite literally. Just as the concerned hen gathers her chicks under her wings[20] in a moment of danger and covers them, laying down her life rather than depriving them of this hiding place that makes it impossible for the enemy's eye to discover them, in the same way he hides your sin. In the same way, for he is also concerned, infinitely concerned in love; he would rather lay down his life than deprive you of your safe hiding place under his love. He would rather lay down his life—yet no, precisely for this reason he laid down his life, in order to secure a hiding place for you under his love. And for this reason also—not in the same way as the hen, that is, only in the same way as or infinitely more concerned than the hen covers its chicks, but otherwise not in the same way; for he hides with *his death*. Oh eternally secure, oh blessedly secured hiding place! For the chicks there is still one danger; although hidden, they are still constantly in danger. When the mother has done the utmost, out of love has laid down her life for them, then the hiding place is taken away from them. But he, on the contrary—yes, if he covered your sin with his life, then there would indeed be the possibility of the danger that they would deprive him of life and you of the hiding place. It is different when he covers your sin with his death; he would rather—if it were necessary, if everything were not decided with the one time[21]—he would rather lay down his life once again in order to procure by his death a hiding place for you than have you deprived of the hiding place. He covers your sin quite literally, precisely because he hides it with his death. Death can of course take away a living person, but it is impossible to take away a dead person, and thus impossible for you to be deprived of your hiding place. If justice were then to fly into a rage, what more

20. See Matthew 23:37.
21. See Hebrews 7:27, 9:12, 25–26, 28, 10:10–14.

does it want than the death penalty; but it has indeed been paid, his death is your hiding place. What infinite love! There is talk of works of love, and many such can be mentioned.[22] But when there is talk of love's work or good work, then there is, yes, then there is only one work, and oddly enough, then you also know at once whom the talk is about, about him, about Jesus Christ, about his atoning death, which hides a multitude of sins.

This is proclaimed at the altar; for from the pulpit it is essentially his life that is proclaimed, but at the altar it is his death. He died once for the sins of the whole world and for our sins; his death is not repeated but *this* is repeated: he died also for you, you who in his body and blood receive the pledge that he has died also for you, at the altar, where he gives you *himself* as a hiding place. Oh secure hiding place for the sinner, oh blessed hiding place, especially after first having learned what it means when the conscience accuses, and the law judges, and justice punitively prosecutes, then, exhausted to the point of despair, to find rest in the only hiding place that is to be found! A human being, even the most loving, can at most give you mitigation, extenuation, leaving it to you whether you can now use it—but he cannot give you himself. Only Jesus Christ can do that; he gives you himself as a hiding place; it is not some grounds of consolation he gives you, not a doctrine he communicates to you, no, he gives you himself. Just as the night spreads, covering everything, so he gave himself[23] and became the hiding place behind which lies a sinful world that he saved. Through this hiding place justice makes its way, not merely toned down, as when the sun's rays break through colored glass; no, impotently it breaks against this hiding place and does not break through. He gave himself for the whole world as a hiding place, also for you just as for me.

Therefore my Lord and Savior, you whose love hides a multitude of sins, when I am quite sensible of my sin and the multitude of my sins, when before justice in heaven there is only wrath over me and over my life, when on earth there is only one person I hate and detest, one person I would flee, even if it were to the ends of the earth,[24] in order to avoid myself—then I will not begin the futile attempt that surely only leads either deeper into despair or to madness, but I will flee at

22. See WL, 3.
23. See Galatians 2:20.
24. See Psalm 139:9.

once to you, and you will not deny me the hiding place you have lovingly offered to all; you will screen me from the eyes of justice, rescue me from this person and from the recollection with which he tortures me; you will help me to dare, by becoming a changed, a different, a better person, to remain in my hiding place, forgotten by justice and by that person whom I detest.

Attentive listener, it is to the love that hides a multitude of sins you go today, seeking it at the altar. From the church's servant you have received assurance of the gracious forgiveness of your sins; you receive the pledge of that at the altar. And not only that, for you not only receive this pledge just as you can receive a pledge from a human being that he bears this feeling for you or this attitude toward you, no, you receive the pledge as a pledge that you receive [Christ] himself; as you receive the pledge, you receive [Christ] himself, in and with the visible sign he gives you himself as a cover over your sins. As he is the truth,[25] you do not then come to know what truth is from him and now are left to yourself, but only remain in the truth by remaining in him.[26] As he is the way, you do not then come to know from him what way you must go and now, left to yourself, must go your own way, but only by remaining in him do you remain on the way. As he is the life, you do not then have life handed over by him and now must shift for yourself, but only by remaining in him do you have life[27]—in this way he is also the hiding place; only by remaining in him, only by identifying yourself with him are you in hiding and there is a cover over the multitude of your sins. For that reason the Lord's Supper is called communion with him.[28] It is not merely in remembrance of him, not merely a pledge that you have communion with him, but it is the communion, this communion that you then must strive to preserve in your daily life by living more and more out of yourself and identifying yourself with him,[29] with his love, which hides a multitude of sins.

25. See John 14:6.
26. See John 8:31.
27. See John 6:56–58, 15:4–8.
28. See 1 Corinthians 10:16.
29. See Galatians 2:19–20.

INDEX

~

Currently a Scholar in Residence at Stetson University, **Sylvia Walsh** is the author of three books on Kierkegaard; the translator and co-editor of his most famous work, *Fear and Trembling;* the co-editor of a collection of feminist interpretations of Kierkegaard; and the author of many published articles and papers presented at national and international conferences. She has served twice as president of the Søren Kierkegaard Society in the United States and is a member of the advisory board of the International Kierkegaard Commentary.